Knowing God's Triune Story

Michael Lindvall

Knowing God's Triune Story

Publisher
Joseph D. Small

Editors
Frank T. Hainer
Mark D. Hinds

Writer
Michael Lindvall

Study Sessions
Starr Luteri

Cover Design
Meredith Gruebbel

Published by Witherspoon Press, a ministry of the General Assembly Mission Council, Presbyterian Church (U.S.A.), 100 Witherspoon St., Louisville, Kentucky.

PRINTED IN THE UNITED STATES OF AMERICA

pcusa.org/witherspoon

Introduction

"Back to basics" is one of the bywords of our time. At best, it is a popular cry for clear thinking about the things that matter most.

Occasionally, however, "back to basics" suggests an anti-intellectual avoidance of hard thinking about anything, even things that matter. Many people today classify the Trinity with all of those elusive abstractions that are both too hard to think about and not obviously relevant for day-to-day living. The doctrine of the Trinity asks for some hard thinking, but it is thinking about things that matter in a way that matters.

Too often the Trinity has been relegated to the rarefied atmosphere of abstract speculation about the inner life of God. Our understanding of the Trinity is a narrative understanding; that is, we understand God through God's storied actions with us and on our behalf. God's self-communication in Jesus Christ through the power of the Holy Spirit is who God is in God's self. Thus, we do not have to speculate about the inner life of God, for the God we see is the One who is.

The venerable doctrine of the Trinity has enjoyed a renaissance among theologians over the last few decades, but that renewed interest has only seldom trickled down into the pews of our churches. My goals in this little book are two, both straightforward—first, to explore the depths of the doctrine in a way that is accessible to the average reader without trivializing its subtleties; and, second, to share my conviction that the Trinity is not just true and interesting, but profoundly important to how Christians believe in God and how they live their lives.

The Story of God

Day 1
From the *Study Catechism*[1]

Question 1. What is God's purpose for your life?

God wills that I should live by the grace of the Lord Jesus Christ, for the love of God, and in the communion of the Holy Spirit.

> *2 Cor. 13:13 "The grace of the Lord Jesus Christ, the love of God, and the communion of the Holy Spirit be with all of you."*

Question 2. How do you live by the grace of the Lord Jesus Christ?

I am not my own. I have been bought with a price. The Lord Jesus Christ loved me and gave himself for me. I entrust myself completely to his care, giving thanks each day for his wonderful goodness.

> *1 Cor. 6:19–20 "You are not your own for you were bought with a price"*

> *Gal. 2:20 "And the life I now live in the flesh I live by faith in the Son of God, who loved me and gave himself for me."*

> *Ps. 136:1 "O give thanks to the Lord, for he is good, for his steadfast love endures forever."*

Question 3. How do you live for the love of God?

I love because God first loved me. God loves me in Christ with a love that never ends. Amazed by grace, I no longer live for myself. I live for the Lord who died and rose again, triumphant over death, for my

---

1. *Study Catechism: Full Version with Biblical References*. Approved by the 210th General Assembly (1998) of the Presbyterian Church (U.S.A.)

sake. Therefore, I take those around me to heart, especially those in particular need, knowing that Christ died for them no less than for me.

1 John 4:19 "We love because he first loved us."

2 Cor. 5:15 "And he died for all, so that those who live might live no longer for themselves, but for him who died and was raised for them."

Rom. 12:15–16 "Rejoice with those who rejoice, weep with those who weep. Live in harmony with one another; do not be haughty, but associate with the lowly; do not claim to be wiser than you are."

Question 4. How do you live in the communion of the Holy Spirit?

By the Holy Spirit, I am made one with the Lord Jesus Christ. I am baptized into Christ's body, the church, along with all others who confess him by faith. As a member of this community, I trust in God's Word, share in the Lord's Supper, and turn to God constantly in prayer. As I grow in grace and knowledge, I am led to do the good works that God intends for my life.

1 Cor. 12:27 "Now you are the body of Christ and individually members of it."

Gal. 3:27 "As many of you as were baptized into Christ have clothed yourselves with Christ."

1 Cor. 6:17, 19 "But anyone united to the Lord becomes one spirit with him. Or do you not know that your body is a temple of the Holy Spirit within you, which you have from God?"

2 Pet. 3:18 "But grow in the grace and knowledge of our Lord and Savior Jesus Christ."

Eph. 2:10 "For we are what he has made us, created in Christ Jesus for good works, which God prepared beforehand to be our way of life."

Truth and Truths

For my thoughts are not your thoughts,

nor are your ways my ways, says the Lord.

For as the heavens are higher than the earth,

so are my ways higher than your ways

and my thoughts than your thoughts.

—Isaiah 55:8–9

We Presbyterians trust that God has spoken and acted. God has reached into our time and space, revealing—speaking—truth about God's self, about ourselves, and about the world. This truth is not relative to our current opinions and personal perspectives. Even if such divine speech and activity are not always easy to discern and to understand, we trust that God has spoken and acted.

Our thoughts and language about God are not mere speculation; they are based in what God has done in history: the story of Israel; the life, death, and resurrection of Jesus Christ; and in our own experience with the living God. Our Reformed tradition has challenged church folks to place their minds in service of the faith, to reason together. God has come near and is readily accessible for our devotion, including our systematic thought. However, the Reformed tradition has also been stubborn in reminding us that words can never capture or hold the sovereign God fast, however eloquent or reasoned. God cannot be boxed up and served in concepts, however well-conceived.

We name our thinking and talking about God "theology," and the truths we speak about God we often call "doctrine," at least when there is some consensus. Theological truths are not all equal in the height or depth of their truth.

Truth, at least theological truth, is like a pyramid. At the bottom are a great many things that are said to be true, but these abundant lower truths are not as unequivocally true or as important as those true things that are farther up the pyramid. Halfway up the pyramid are fewer truths, but these truths are more clearly true or more important in their truth. At the sharp peak of the pyramid are the very few and the very important truths. Perhaps at the very pinnacle there is one nearly perfect truth of inestimable and incomparable importance.

This image of theological truth as a pyramid is different from the post-modern idea of relative truth, which says that all truth is relative to each person, and as such, changes simply because truth is based largely on the differing experiences, perspectives, and opinions of individuals rather than on external reality. In such a view, there is little or no absolute or eternal truth. The only real credo of such relativism may be: What is true for me is not necessarily true for you. I contend that theological truths are relative to one another. This is not the same thing as saying that they are merely relative to us. Some theological dicta are indeed truer, more important, and more compelling than others. That is to say, some are nearer to the top of the pyramid.

Such relativism runs counter to our trust that God has somehow spoken and acted. God has reached into our time and space, revealing—speaking truth about God's self, about the world, and about ourselves. This truth is not relative to our current opinions and personal perspectives.

Three-Part Movement

"I am the Alpha and the Omega," says the Lord God, who is and who was and who is to come, the Almighty.

—Revelation 1:8

Imagine a three-part movement that outlines in a general way how we know things. This three-movement progression is not my invention, but I would like to expand on it in a way that I hope will help us to better understand how the Trinity is not only truth, but also important truth.

The first movement of the three is experience itself. This first movement is the eternally immediate moment—the "right now." It is the very passing of moment to moment that is living. It is the seeing and touching and hearing and tasting of things in themselves. For example, the first movement was whatever occurred when Moses encountered the divine in the experience of the burning bush. This first movement was the actual Jesus encountered by his disciples, paralytics, and outcast women in dusty Galilean towns.

This first movement is the actual experience I had of eating my breakfast and drinking my coffee this morning. And all such experience is forever passing from immediacy into memory in a flash—flash upon flash. Experience becomes memory in no time, and then each ensuing experience is itself seen through the lens of memory. Later experience is understood in terms of the understanding that the earlier experience has created and of the expectations that memory has planted. Experience is the first component of the three-part movement.

The second component is remembering, thinking about, telling about, and writing the story of the experience. It may or may not be much of a story when I tell you what I had for breakfast; it depends, I suppose, on how well I tell it. But whether it be my description of breakfast, or the story of Moses and the burning bush in the third chapter of Exodus, or the story of Jesus in the four Gospels, this remembering and relating the experience is not the precise re-creation of the actual experience itself. Words are not eggs. Words are not a burning bush. Words are not Jesus. Nevertheless, this act of remembering is central to our being.

Our stories define us. Most of the Bible belongs to this second movement, the movement of remembering what happened and telling the story of it. The great preponderance of its pages are narrative, the inspired, written story that remembers the experiences people had with God. The story is the second movement.

The third movement of the three is abstraction. This is the drawing of conclusions, the writing of declarative sentences that summarize, categorize, conclude, and state the meaning of what is remembered in the second movement. Here lies most theology; here lie doctrine, philosophy, and ethics. The truth is, there is not nearly as much religious abstraction in the Bible as there is narrative. Perhaps two-thirds of its pages are the telling of the stories of what happened. Scripture is not so much doctrine, theology, or ethics as it is simply the remembering and the retelling of the story of people's experiences with the living God.

But it is God who establishes us with you in Christ and has anointed us, by putting his seal on us and giving us his Spirit in our hearts as a first installment.

—2 Corinthians 1:21–22

Consider an example of this three-part progression of understanding: First, there was the Jesus of history who walked Galilean roads and spoke Aramaic. This is the Jesus encountered by Peter and James and the Samaritan woman at the well. Second, there are the four Gospels, creatively told stories about Jesus in which the truth of the experiences that people had with this man is told for others so they might understand both the original experience and Jesus.

The Gospels reveal in powerfully emblematic ways the truth about the experiences of those who knew Jesus. Part of the experience was that they recognized that God was in Jesus in a singular way. They who had these experiences and told the story of them recognized that Jesus was God in a way that exploded their paradigms. Such a statement is a theological affirmation; it is not narrative. It is a conclusion, the third of this three-part movement, the component that draws concept from story. In this example, the experience people had of the divine that they recognized in Jesus became the gospel story, which contains and leads to the doctrine they drew from the story.

The early church teachers and the councils took up the work of theology, ethics, and the development of consensus theology (doctrine) boldly. Beginning with the Jesus of experience the church captured those experiences in story form and extracted theological statements about Jesus from those stories. In this third step, theology carves the sharp-cornered forms of doctrine out of the fluid story. The church develops the doctrine of the incarnation from the story of the Gospels. The doctrinal formulation is the third movement.

This third movement is by definition inductive, generalized, analytical, and reductionist. Abstraction is needful in some teaching, and is especially important for thinking systematically. Abstraction sets parameters and often serves to clarify obscurity. But remember: No concept, no abstraction, no theology is ever the same thing as the story that it conceptualizes, abstracts, or theologizes. The story is always more than any or all of the conceptual truths we may abstract from it.

Abstract truth born in this third movement is not by dint of its position any truer than the truth contained in artful storytelling or good painting or music. The doctrine of the incarnation is not truer than the story of the nativity. Theology is not truer than Scripture. Both are true, but for different purposes and in different ways. Theology moves properly from the basis of Scripture, but should always be well-rooted in the story Scripture tells.

Three-Storied Story

When words are many, transgression is not lacking, but the prudent are restrained in speech.

—Proverbs 10:19

What then, you may ask, has all of this to do with the doctrine of the Trinity? Just this: The understanding of God as Father, Son, and Holy Spirit is not so much an abstraction; that is, it does not belong so much to the third movement described previously. Rather, even though we call the Trinity a doctrine, it belongs as much or more to the second movement. The Trinity is a story about God more than an abstraction about God. I invite you to begin to understand the Trinity by approaching it as a very condensed version of the story of the Bible. For Christians, Scripture is the great story of God's way with us. The Trinity is the radically abbreviated story of God's way with us.

Once upon a time there was a great emperor who sought wisdom. He gathered all the great scholars of the empire and charged them to write down all the wisdom of the world so that he might read it and become wise. After ten years, they came back with a veritable library, dozens of volumes. Seeing all of those words, the emperor said, "Shorter, please." Several years later they returned with just one book. Again the emperor said, "Shorter, please." In time they returned with but a page, then a paragraph. But the emperor, wanting his truth even pithier, sent them back yet again. This last time they returned with but a sentence. The emperor unfolded the piece of paper on which the scholars had condensed all the wisdom of the world and read "There is no such thing as a free lunch."

In a very real sense, the early church did much the same thing. In the first four centuries of the church's life, faithful Christians who knew the story (and not just theologians) condensed the great story of Scripture in a way that identified and named the God of the Bible. This radically brief but accurate condensation of the story affirms that God came, and yet comes, to us as Father, Son, and Holy Spirit. The church did this not so much to simplify as to offer a concise vocabulary with which to accurately speak the truth about and worship the God of Scripture. This is to say, if we were to speak of God only as Father, our understanding of the God of the Bible would be incomplete. Likewise, if we were to speak of God only as Jesus Christ or the Holy Spirit, the story of God would be told incompletely.

The three persons of this one God do not reveal themselves in the Bible in a one, two, three order. In the Old Testament, the people of Israel experienced God largely as what Christians would call the first person of the Trinity. But we must also remember that in the first chapter of Genesis, "the Spirit of God was moving over the waters." And again and again, it is the Spirit—in Hebrew, *ruach*, or Breath or Wind of God—who inspires prophets or who rests (or does not rest) upon assorted rulers.

In the creation story, God "speaks" creation into being (*Gen. 1*). God's Word is a creative agent, the expression of God. Trinitarian theology connects this expressive aspect of God with the second person of the Trinity.

Day 6
God's Enduring Word

In the beginning was the Word, and the Word was with God, and the Word was God. . . . All things came into being through him, and without him not one thing came into being. . . .

—John 1:1, 3

The first chapter of John, on the edge of poetry, uses extensively the Greek word for "word," *logos*. In that familiar passage, the Word is first identified as the dynamic expression of God in the act of creation. A few verses later, John identifies the same Word, or *logos*, as God's expression of the divine self in Jesus Christ.

But the expression of God found in the Gospels does not stop with Jesus Christ, the second person of the Trinity. All four Gospels present a relationship, a relationship of deepest love and intimacy, between Jesus and the God he calls Father. The very word that Jesus uses for Father, the Aramaic term *Abba,* is much more intimate than the rather formal English word Father. Odd as it rings in our ears, Abba may be closer to Daddy.

And the Holy Spirit does not wait until Pentecost to make an appearance in the New Testament. The Spirit comes upon Mary as Jesus is conceived in her womb. The Spirit descends upon Jesus at his baptism. In the fourth chapter of Luke, Jesus reads these words from the prophet Isaiah to his hometown synagogue: "The Spirit of the Lord is upon me . . . ." And after Pentecost, when the Holy Spirit becomes an even more important presence in the story, the Spirit is always connected to Jesus and the God whom Jesus called Father.

The Trinity is not a three-stage revelation. True, the Gospels do focus on Jesus, and the Old Testament witnesses to the God whom Christians name the first person of the Trinity. And it is true that the Holy Spirit comes to prominence in the story of the church after Pentecost. Nevertheless, the God who is Trinity is always Trinity—even from the beginning. And the God at the end of the story has become not just the Holy Spirit, but is God in three persons, the God of the whole story.

The Oneness of the Trinity

There is one body and one Spirit, just as you were called to the one hope of your calling, one Lord, one faith, one baptism, one God and Father of all, who is above all and through all and in all.

—Ephesians 4:4–6

Christians, like all human beings, are tempted to tell only part of the story. Unitarianism is a word that is usually used to describe any theology that denies the Trinity altogether. But some theologians have talked about a less radical, "de facto" kind of unitarianism that otherwise traditional Christians have often slipped into when their thinking and their worship become myopically focused on one person of the Trinity to the neglect of the others.

The doctrine of the Trinity guards against distorting our concept of God. Small gods become, at their most benign, shadow gods, tamed and domesticated deities. At their worst, little gods become dead gods or even dangerous. If, for example, faith focuses only on the first person of the Trinity—call this unitarianism of the Father—our picture of God will be incomplete, perhaps even distorted, tending to emphasize God's austerity and judgment.

Further, a unitarianism of the first person of the Trinity could lead to an emphasis on the unknowability of God, leaving us with a speculative God of pure being, a God utterly beyond time and space. In the end, such theology may conclude that little or nothing can be known of God, a position not far from agnosticism. One thinks of Aristotle's Unmoved Mover. Closer to our time, we encounter the unitarianism of the Father implicit in the deism of the Enlightenment. Certain contemporary theologies that disconnect God from the historical Jesus and from the living and active Holy Spirit speculate (often very romantically) about a God of nature, either far removed from our time and space, or so much in everything as to be nothing.

Faith that is too focused on the second person of the Trinity can slip into a shortsighted view of Jesus. Without the first person, that mysterious

God of pure being, people forget the truth that God is radically other. Such unitarianism of the second person often reduces God to a cozy friend, a meek and mild God-as-just-Jesus. The God of the universe, mighty and mysterious, the giver of the law, the God of the prophets who demands justice, may recede far into the background. The "Jesus freaks" of the sixties often operated in a unitarianism of the second person, fascinated, as they were, with Jesus, but attending little to the God of the universe or to the intimate presence of God in the Holy Spirit.

Unitarianism of the third person, which many observers believe is the trend in our day, focuses intently on one's own immediate, personal, and subjective experience of God in the Spirit. Pentecostalism, which sometimes tends to this kind of unitarianism, is one of the fastest growing expressions of Christianity in the world. Such Spirit-focused faith tends to see God as the one who can be known in the depths of personal experience. In the extremes of such unitarianism of the Spirit, the believer's own personal and subjective experience of God in the Spirit becomes the norm. Both the God of mystery and the God of history are nudged off the stage and into the wings.

Our task is to tell the whole story of God, to praise God in God's Trinitarian completeness. As a stool needs three legs to stand, so does our doctrine of God.

 Write one question about this week's readings you would like to ask your study group.

The Story of God

Main Idea

The doctrine of the Trinity is a radical but accurate condensation of the full Bible story.

Preparing to Lead

- Read the daily readings for Days 1–7.
- Read through this session and choose activities and discussion topics. Be open to asking questions that arise from your reading of the book.
- Several days prior to the group meeting, assign various participants words or phrases from the following list to define. Invite the participants to be prepared to share their definitions.

  ❏ Experience
  ❏ Story
  ❏ Abstraction
  ❏ Paradigm
  ❏ "Thinking systematically"
  ❏ Parameters
  ❏ Inductive
  ❏ Analytical

Opening Activities

- Welcome: As group members arrive, extend words and gestures of welcome. Consider providing name tags and pens. Give some thought to asking another group member to provide refreshments.
- Opening prayer: After a brief time of informal conversation, invite the group members to join in prayer.

Guiding the Discussion

- Sketch a pyramid on poster board or newsprint. Encourage participants to place the components of the following list on the pyramid according to the components' relative importance in their own faith and experience. Retain the pyramid to discuss it again in Session Five.

  ❑ Trinity
  ❑ Incarnation
  ❑ Forgiveness
  ❑ Ascension of Christ
  ❑ Creation
  ❑ Sanctification
  ❑ God's love
  ❑ Justification
  ❑ God with us
  ❑ Resurrection

- Working in small groups, if feasible, write the abstract concept illustrated in the following stories, using a few words for each concept.

  ❑ Weeds in the wheat   Matthew 13:24–30
  ❑ Pearl of great value   Matthew 13:45–46
  ❑ The sheep and goats   Matthew 25:31–46
  ❑ Widow's offering   Mark 12:41–44
  ❑ The lost coin   Luke 15:8–10
  ❑ Shepherd and sheep   John 10:1–39
  ❑ Vine and branches   John 15:1–27

- Engage participants in a discussion of the "three-movement progression" in the following story:

  > Jamie was standing beside the road when a stray dog ran into the path of a car. Running as fast as he could, the four-year-old hurried to tell his mother that he had seen the driver stop and that the dog had run away, apparently unhurt. His mother hugged Jamie as he said, "I'm never, ever going to run into the street, never, ever."

Determine the "three-movement progression" in Jamie's "knowing": What was Jamie's actual experience? What was his story? What abstract concept did he perceive?

- Read through Luke 24:28–35. Sort out the three "movements" in the progression: the experience, the story about the experience, and the abstract concept. How does the Gospel writer define the concept for the reader? Compare Luke 18:31–34; 19:11–27; and 20:20–26.

- Explain to the participants that the abstract concept "God is forgiving" could be told as the story of the prodigal son. With what biblical stories could each of the following concepts be told? (There may be more than one correct answer to each.)

    - ❏ God answers prayer.
    - ❏ Forgive one another.
    - ❏ Justice eventually will be given.
    - ❏ Generosity is rewarded.
    - ❏ Care for strangers.

Concluding the Session

- Invite participants to share family stories and to explore the "three-movement progression" in those stories: experience, story, and abstraction. Remember that this is a time for sharing and affirmation, not for discussion or critique of anybody's story.
- Using hymnals look up the hymn "Come, Thou Almighty King." How does this hymn express the doctrine of the Trinity? What do worshipers learn about the Trinity as they sing this hymn?

Notes:

God Is as God Does

Day 8
John 3:1-17

Now there was a Pharisee named Nicodemus, a leader of the Jews. He came to Jesus by night and said to him, "Rabbi, we know that you are a teacher who has come from God; for no one can do these signs that you do apart from the presence of God." Jesus answered him, "Very truly, I tell you, no one can see the kingdom of God without being born from above." Nicodemus said to him, "How can anyone be born after having grown old? Can one enter a second time into the mother's womb and be born?" Jesus answered, "Very truly, I tell you, no one can enter the kingdom of God without being born of water and Spirit. What is born of the flesh is flesh, and what is born of the Spirit is spirit. Do not be astonished that I said to you, 'You must be born from above.' The wind blows where it chooses, and you hear the sound of it, but you do not know where it comes from or where it goes. So it is with everyone who is born of the Spirit." Nicodemus said to him, "How can these things be?" Jesus answered him, "Are you a teacher of Israel, and yet you do not understand these things?

"Very truly, I tell you, we speak of what we know and testify to what we have seen; yet you do not receive our testimony. If I have told you about earthly things and you do not believe, how can you believe if I tell you about heavenly things? No one has ascended into heaven except the one who descended from heaven, the Son of Man. And just as Moses lifted up the serpent in the wilderness, so must the Son of Man be lifted up, that whoever believes in him may have eternal life.

"For God so loved the world that he gave his only Son, so that everyone who believes in him may not perish but may have eternal life.

"Indeed, God did not send the Son into the world to condemn the world, but in order that the world might be saved through him."

Prayer:
> Father, we praise you;
> through your Word and Holy Spirit you created all things.
> You reveal your salvation in all the world
> by sending to us Jesus Christ, the Word made flesh.
> Through your Holy Spirit
> you give us a share in your life and love.
> Fill us with the vision of your glory,
> that we may always serve and praise you,
> Father, Son, and Holy Spirit,
> one God, forever and ever. Amen.[1]

---

1. *Book of Common Worship* (Louisville: Westminster John Knox Press, 1993), p. 349. Reprinted with permission of the Office of the General Assembly.

Knowing God's Triune Story

A Short Version of a Long Story

Long ago God spoke to our ancestors in many and various ways by the prophets, but in these last days he has spoken to us by a Son, whom he appointed heir of all things, through whom he also created the worlds. He is the reflection of God's glory and the exact imprint of God's very being, and he sustains all things by his powerful word. When he had made purification for sins, he sat down at the right hand of the Majesty on high, having become as much superior to angels as the name he has inherited is more excellent than theirs.

—Hebrews 1:1–4

I have asked you to begin thinking about the Trinity in a way that, for most of us, represents a subtle paradigm shift. I have challenged you to begin thinking of the Trinity not so much as an abstract idea, but as first and most simply a radical condensation of a very long story. The Bible, this book at the center of our faith, is not essentially a book of concepts, but rather a book of remembered experiences and stories that together form the great story of God's self-revelation. This great story includes the stories of Israel, the story of Jesus of Nazareth, and, finally, the story of the men and women who followed Jesus and became the church of the New Testament. Christians have often been tempted to condense this great story inaccurately, de-emphasizing one part, perhaps omitting it altogether, or focusing myopically on just one portion of a very great narrative.

The Trinity works to safeguard the entirety and integrity of the whole drama of salvation, condensing it, as it were. The Trinity holds stubbornly before us the whole truth of the story we remember, tell, and live out. The Trinity tells us that we have known God in three persons, and here I fall back on spatial vocabulary, as inadequate as any words about God, but helpful nonetheless:

The first person of the Trinity is God "above," the Creator God, the God of Israel, the God whom Jesus calls Abba.

The second person of the Trinity is God "alongside us" in the creative *logos*, fully expressed in Jesus Christ.

The third person of the Trinity is God "in us," as a Spirit we name Holy, God present in human hearts and active in human communities, God in the present tense.

The Trinity is a short version of a long story articulated to guard the completeness of the great story. The Trinity is even more than a story radically condensed. The Trinity is also an idea, a verbal image for God. I would go further and say that the Trinity is a way that faithful Christians have long taken to journey more deeply into God.

A Parable

He said to them, "Is a lamp brought in to be put under the bushel basket, or under the bed, and not on the lampstand? For there is nothing hidden, except to be disclosed; nor is anything secret, except to come to light. Let anyone with ears to hear listen!"

—Mark 4:21–23

Every year a family went different directions on Christmas Eve. The mother and children went faithfully to church to celebrate the miracle of God's coming to be one with us in Christ. The father of the family, however, was a good-hearted but stubborn skeptic who was unable to reconcile his doubts about this central mystery of the Christian faith with church attendance, even on Christmas Eve. He invariably stayed home and kept the night in his own way. Every year, he built a fire in the living room fireplace and read until his family returned.

One Christmas Eve saw his family set off into an especially cold night, the sky heavy with threatened snow. As the evening wore on, the weather turned ever grimmer: first came snow, and then a cold, howling wind, and then even more bitter cold. Settled with his book, the father suddenly heard a thump against the picture window opposite the blazing fire. Then there was another, and yet another. He left his chair to investigate, and discovered that a flock of birds, confused and frightened by the storm, had apparently seen the light of his fire and were trying to fly to it through the large window. Several lay stunned in the snow. A compassionate man, he donned his coat and boots, lit a lantern, and left the warmth of his living room to go out into the storm to see if he could help the birds to safety.

He opened the large door on his garage and set the lantern against the back wall, hoping the light would attract the birds as the fire in the fireplace had. Standing at the entrance, he waved his arms toward the lantern and exhorted the birds to go to safety in the garage. But the birds were confused by his immense and intimidating form, frightened of his flailing arms and strange, deep cries. He then stepped aside, hiding in the darkness at the side of the garage, but still the birds were too afraid and disoriented to go into strange surroundings, even though the garage was safe and dry.

They grew more and more exhausted, their lives now endangered. In his frustration, the man finally said to himself, "If only I could become a bird for just a moment, and lead them to safety." Out of compassion, he wished for an incarnation, as it were, wished to be in a sense what Christians would call "the second person of the Trinity." He wished to be a bird, so that he might show the birds the way to life. In that desperate wish, in his love for these endangered creatures, the logic of the incarnation that had so long eluded him suddenly made sense in a way it had not before.

Why God Became Human

Since, then, we have a great high priest who has passed through the heavens, Jesus, the Son of God, let us hold fast to our confession. For we do not have a high priest who is unable to sympathize with our weaknesses, but we have one who in every respect has been tested as we are, yet without sin. Let us therefore approach the throne of grace with boldness, so that we may receive mercy and find grace to help in time of need.

—Hebrews 4:14–16

The story of the man who would be a bird argues for the necessity of the incarnation. It is a parable of God becoming like us to save us. To do that, the august, mighty God must speak our words, live our life, and suffer our fate. In so doing, God becomes accessible to us. As such, the story illumines in a simple way the Word-became-flesh, the second person of the Trinity.

The story illustrates another important aspect of Trinitarian thinking. If the man in the story had actually been able to become a bird for a wistful moment, able to communicate with the other birds, he would have retained the same intent, compassion, care, and love that he had as a human being. This is to say, he would as a bird accurately represent what he was as a human. He would not have misrepresented himself.

In the same way, Jesus is God in that his words, compassion, life, death, and resurrection accurately represent God to us. In other words, there is not some other hidden God behind Jesus who is essentially different from the God whom we encounter in Jesus. This is not to say that Jesus as we encounter him exhausts the total meaning and mystery of God. Rather, it says that he is "the truth" in that he does not present a false image or a radically incomplete image of God's mystery.

For a long time, theologians have distinguished two ways to speak about the Trinity: the immanent and the economic Trinity. The immanent Trinity might be called the inner being of God, even the nature of God. It refers to what God is in God's self. The economic Trinity refers to the way of God with us, the external shape of our experience with God over time. This is God-with-us personally in our individual lives and together in our communities. The economic Trinity speaks of what God does in relationship to us in the world.

Essential to the integrity of faith and theology is the affirmation that the God of the immanent Trinity is the same as the God of the economic Trinity. That is to say, God is as God does. The expressive economic Trinity of history and experience adequately represents the internal reality of God, the immanent Trinity. If we fail to trust in substantial correspondence between these two ways of speaking and thinking of God, we have a problem. That is, if we fail to trust that the God revealed in Scripture and in our lives truly reflects who God actually is, we come to an impasse.

Without this correspondence between the doings of the God of history, and the being of the eternal, transcendent God, then human beings can know nothing whatsoever about God.

Augustine on the Trinity

Beloved, let us love one another, because love is from God; everyone who loves is born of God and knows God. Whoever does not love does not know God, for God is love. God's love was revealed among us in this way: God sent his only Son into the world so that we might live through him. In this is love, not that we loved God but that he loved us and sent his Son to be the atoning sacrifice for our sins. Beloved, since God loved us so much, we also ought to love one another.

—1 John 4:7–11

The God we have experienced in history, who acts out love and justice, who incarnates compassion and mercy, is precisely the same creative power behind the universe. There is no hidden God in the sense that there is a different God behind the God of history and experience. This point may seem at first glance little more than a theological curiosity. But the truth is, this affirmation of the continuity between God as God is and God as God does is radically practical and of crucial importance. It means that God is not some unknowable mystery only vaguely hinted at in Scripture and human experience. It means that the one who is the center of the cosmos, the one who is source and end of all things, the one who is "all in all" is the very same God who led an ancient tribe of Semitic slaves to freedom. It means that the lord of the universe is the very Jesus who healed the lame and took little children onto his knees.

The deepest things are not totally hidden in a mist of mystery, but are made known to us in what God has done and is doing among us. Acts of love and mercy reveal a God of love and mercy. If what God has done dependably corresponds to who God is, it means that at the very heart of the universe lie love, mercy, grace, truth, and righteousness. This is truth that matters.

St. Augustine of Hippo, numbered among the greatest of the church's theologians, lived in North Africa in the fourth century at the historical intersection of the fading classical Greco-Roman world and the tumultuous, emerging Christian world. His important discussion of the immanent Trinity focuses on an analysis of love. Love implies a lover, the beloved, and their mutual love. He argues for a threefold understanding of the Godhead in terms of Father, Son, and Holy Spirit.

God's nature is relational. This applies not only to creation, but also immanently—that is, in God's internal self insofar as such is imaginable to us. All relationships are in three parts: two persons and the life or personality of their relationship. God's nature is relationship, Augustine affirms: the one who loves, the one who is loved, and the love that animates the relationship. And, as we shall explore in the next session, God is love (*1 John 4:8*), the Lover corresponding to God the Father, the Beloved corresponding to God the Son, and the Love that unites them corresponding to God the Holy Spirit. The four Gospels, remember, present us not simply with a picture of Jesus, but rather with a portrait of a relationship between Jesus and the God he calls Father. And it is the Spirit who breathes life into relationships.

Sayers on the Trinity

Then Jesus came from Galilee to John at the Jordan, to be baptized by him. John would have prevented him, saying, "I need to be baptized by you, and do you come to me?" But Jesus answered him, "Let it be so now; for it is proper for us in this way to fulfill all righteousness." Then he consented. And when Jesus had been baptized, just as he came up from the water, suddenly the heavens were opened to him and he saw the Spirit of God descending like a dove and alighting on him. And a voice from heaven said, "This is my Son, the Beloved, with whom I am well pleased."

—Matthew 3:13–17

Dorothy Sayers, best known as the creator of the Lord Peter Wimsey mystery novels, was also something of an early feminist. A devout Christian, she was skeptical of people who said they wanted deep faith without deep thought.

Sayers presents an economic Trinity, arguing that the essential three-ness of God is reflected in all action and creativity. In her play *The Zeal for Thy House,* she has the archangel Michael make this fine speech: "For every work (or act) of creation is threefold, an earthly trinity to match the heavenly. First . . . there is the Creative Idea, passionless, timeless, beholding the whole work complete at once, the end in the beginning: and this is the image of the Father. Second, there is the Creative . . . Activity begotten of that idea, working in time from the beginning to the end, with sweat and passion, being incarnate in the bonds of matter: and this is the image of the Word. Third, there is the Creative Power, the meaning of the work and its response in the lively soul: and this is the image of the indwelling Spirit."[1]

Sayers explains her point by using an activity she knows well: the act of a creative artist, specifically the act of writing a book.[2] First, she says, there is the idea for the book.

1. Dorothy L. Sayers, *The Mind of the Maker* (San Francisco: Continuum International Publishing Group, 2004), p. 28.
2. Ibid., *passim.*

The idea, the content of the book, exists only in the writer's head. Nobody else can see it or know anything about it. It is pure being, pure thought, reality, a mystery known only to itself in the same way that the first person of the Trinity is God in divine reality, unknown and unknowable.

But then, she goes on, when the book is written, when the idea is put down on paper, when it exists in space and time, idea becomes *logos*, the word, a living expression that reveals the pure idea that was in the head of the writer. This book is an incarnate thing; it is ink and paper, just as Jesus Christ was flesh and blood. As *logos*, it faithfully mirrors the pure idea in a way parallel to Christ, who mirrors God as God's self.

But, Sayers continues (and here her analogy finds its true genius), the book is nothing but ink and paper until somebody reads it. Only then does ". . . the written page become power in the mind and imagination of the reader." This corresponds to the Spirit, the immediate and personal experience of the pure idea made incarnate in the book and powerful in the reading of the book.

Day 14
An Icon for God

No one has ever seen God; if we love one another, God lives in us, and his love is perfected in us. By this we know that we abide in him and he in us, because he has given us of his Spirit.

—1 John 4:12–13

At this point, having turned to as unlikely a pair as St. Augustine and Dorothy Sayers to illumine the Trinity, I offer one last fine but most important distinction. "No one has ever seen God" confesses the writer of the first letter of John. This is a blunt reminder that all of these well-turned ideas—though accurate and true—are still not portraits of God. Eastern Orthodox Christians make this point in the way they approach icons. An icon, they insist, is not a portrayal of God or even of a saintly person, much less a holy thing to be worshiped for itself. Rather, they insist, an icon is an image that the faithful look through to see into a God who cannot be portrayed. The image leads to God, but is not a precise representation of God.

The Trinity—and for that matter, perhaps all words about God, even Holy Scripture—should function for us in a way analogous to this. The Trinity is an "icon" for God, not because it is a precisely true mathematical or structural diagram of divinity, but because it truly leads one into a deeper, but always imperfect, understanding of God: God whom we have not seen, God whom our minds can never wholly conceive, God whom our words never capture.

I recall how flabbergasted I was when I first learned that scientists had no idea of what an atom looked like. Since the eighth grade I had studied the little diagrams in my science textbooks that showed atoms that looked like little solar systems with electrons buzzing around the complex nuclei like so many planets around the sun—and then to discover that this was no more than a hypothetical picture that explained the facts as we knew them! An atom might well look like this picture, if an atom could ever be seen. But the truth was that the drawings in my science textbooks were no more than representations that illustrated what scientists did know and helped others to understand. No one had ever seen an atom.

An engineer friend offered a similar example in the common understanding most of us have of electricity. "All my life," he said, "I have imagined electricity in the way I was taught. It is like a flowing river. The wider the river, the slower the flow of the stream; the narrower the river, the faster the flow. But electricity isn't a river. In fact, we don't really know exactly how it works. But the river image helps us to understand and imagine it anyway." No one has ever seen electricity, but we dare to describe it with a visual image that truly fits, comprehends, and pictures the truth that we do know.

To guard God's mystery on the one hand and to confess that God is still knowable on the other—this is the theological intersection where all must live out our faith.

 Draw a picture of the author's convictions in this week's readings.

God Is as God Does

Main Idea

The Trinity is more than a condensed story; it is also an image of the reality we know as God.

Preparing to Lead

- Read the daily readings for Days 8–14.
- Read through this session and choose activities and discussion topics. Be open to asking questions that arise from your reading of the book.
- Consider: The concept of the Trinity has been a revered doctrine of the church for centuries; however, it has its limits. Feminist theologians point to the obvious problem that the traditional under-standing of the Trinity leaves no place for any female identification in the Godhead. What other stumbling blocks might one encounter in using the Trinity as a model with which to understand God?
- Several days prior to the group meeting, assign various participants words or phrases from the following list to define. Invite the participants to be prepared to share their definitions.

  ❏ Immanent Trinity
  ❏ Economic Trinity
  ❏ Incarnation
  ❏ Relationship
  ❏ Icon

Opening Activities

- Welcome: As group members arrive, extend words and gestures of welcome. Consider providing name tags and pens. Give some thought to asking another group member to provide refreshments.

- Working in groups to allow each person an opportunity to participate, create models to illustrate the "spatial" description of the Trinity. A stick-figure drawing of a person would be an adequate starting place, but encourage the groups to use their creativity. If time and resources permit, encourage the groups to create models using paint, clay, building blocks, folded paper, and other materials.

- Opening prayer: After giving the groups a chance to share their work, invite the participants to join you in prayer.

Guiding the Discussion

- Review the parable of the man who tried to help the birds. In what ways is the story a good illustration of God's incarnation? In what ways does it fall short of fully representing the gospel message?
- Review Dorothy Sayers's comparison of the Trinity to a writer's concept/printed copy/reader's experience. Would this analogy apply equally well to the process/reality of filmmaking? Video games? Computer software? Other examples?
- Consider that in the Eastern Orthodox Church, an icon is perceived as an image one can "look through" toward God, rather than as a literal portrait of God. The text suggests that the concept of the Trinity and the Scripture itself both should be viewed in the same way. Evaluate this suggestion. How might one "look through" the Scripture toward God without perceiving the Bible as a literal portrait of God?

Concluding the Session

- Collect the following objects (and any others that might be suitable) and set them on a table or tray. Invite participants to choose an object and to use it as a metaphor of the Trinity.

  - ❏ Hard-boiled egg
  - ❏ Glass of water
  - ❏ Apple
  - ❏ Shamrock or clover
  - ❏ Clock face
  - ❏ Quilt

- Guided visualization: Ask someone who enjoys reading aloud to read Psalm 139:1–18. Encourage other participants to relax, close their eyes, and visualize the images evoked by the words of the psalm, remembering that who God is corresponds with what God does. Allow a moment of silence when the reading is completed, then invite group members to share the images and impressions they received. Remember that this is a time for sharing, not for discussion or criticism of others' thoughts.

- Using hymnals, look up the hymn "A Mighty Fortress Is Our God." How does this hymn express the doctrine of the Trinity? What images in the song are consistent with the character of the Creator? Of the Redeemer? Of the Spirit? What do worshipers learn about the Trinity as they sing this hymn?

Notes:

God as Love

Day 15
Luke 4:16-21

When he came to Nazareth, where he had been brought up, he went to the synagogue on the sabbath day, as was his custom. He stood up to read, and the scroll of the prophet Isaiah was given to him. He unrolled the scroll and found the place where it was written: "The Spirit of the Lord is upon me, because he has anointed me to bring good news to the poor. He has sent me to proclaim release to the captives and recovery of sight to the blind, to let the oppressed go free, to proclaim the year of the Lord's favor." And he rolled up the scroll, gave it back to the attendant, and sat down. The eyes of all in the synagogue were fixed on him. Then he began to say to them, "Today this scripture has been fulfilled in your hearing."

Prayer:
>Almighty God,
>you sent Jesus to proclaim your kingdom
>and to teach with authority.
>Anoint us with your Spirit,
>that we too may bring good news to the poor,
>bind up the brokenhearted,
>and proclaim liberty to the captive;
>through Jesus Christ our Lord,
>who lives and reigns with you and the Holy Spirit,
>one God, now and forever. Amen.[1]

---

1. *Book of Common Worship* (Louisville: Westminster John Knox Press, 1993), p. 207. Reprinted with permission of the Office of the General Assembly.

O Lord, our Sovereign,

how majestic is your name in all the earth!

You have set your glory above the heavens.

Out of the mouths of babes and infants

you have founded a bulwark because of your foes,

to silence the enemy and the avenger.

—Psalm 8:1–2

What do you imagine when you say the word *God?* The popular cliché of an old man with a white beard is probably less prevalent in today's world than it was years ago, when stereotypes were more prevalent and language was less inclusive. Philosophers and theologians have shied away from anything so very concrete in talking about God, leaning toward abstractions, often very elusive ones.

Descriptions of God include Unmoved Mover (Aristotle), the Prime Mover (Deists), and Ground of Being (Tillich). Science fiction and popular imagination have created images of God ranging from a stone monolith floating in the dark heart of space to the permeating force diffused in all that lives in the universe.

The Westminster Shorter Catechism is more specific, but still abstract with its magisterial definition of God: "God is a Spirit, infinite, eternal and unchangeable, in his being, wisdom, power, holiness, justice, goodness, and truth."[1]

---

1. *Westminster Shorter Catechism* (7.004), from *The Book of Confessions* (Louisville: Office of the General Assembly, Presbyterian Church [U.S.A.], 2007), p. 175. Reprinted with permission of the Office of the General Assembly.

Knowing God's Triune Story

But what shall we imagine "a Spirit" to be, much less an "infinite, eternal" one? In Aldous Huxley's novel *Those Barren Leaves*, a character named Miss Thriplow who is between affairs and finding herself bored is suddenly taken with the idea that she really ought to become more serious and spiritual. Huxley writes, "She got into bed, and lying on her back, with all her muscles relaxed, she began to think about God . . . God is a spirit, she said to herself, a spirit, a spirit. She tried to picture something huge and empty, but alive. A huge flat expanse of sand, for example, and over it a huge blank dome of sky; and above the sand everything should be tremulous and shimmering with heat—an emptiness that was yet alive. A spirit, an all-pervading spirit. God is a spirit. Three camels appeared on the horizon of the sandy plain and went lolloping along in an absurd, ungainly fashion from left to right. Miss Thriplow made an effort and dismissed them. God is a spirit, she said aloud. But of all animals camels are really almost the queerest; when one thinks of their frightfully supercilious faces, with their protruding underlips like the last Hapsburg kings of Spain . . . No, no; God is a spirit, all-pervading, everywhere. All the universes are made one in him. . . . "[2]

Our mortal minds, shaped as they are by the earthy stuff of daily human experience, long for something solid that the imagination can sink roots into. We are human beings and we think in a human way. Our thoughts are shaped and bounded by what we have seen, heard, smelled, touched, and tasted in the dailiness of life. The vagaries of spirit—without something real to carve that ethereal word into shape—soon devolve into Miss Thriplow's desert with intruding camels or descend to the naïveté of the child's old man in a white beard perched on a cloud.

---

2. Quoted in Robert Clyde Johnson, *The Meaning of Christ*, Layman's Theological Library (Philadelphia: Westminster Press, 1958), p. 10.

God Is Radically Other

Holy, holy, holy is the Lord of hosts;

the whole earth is full of God's glory.

—Isaiah 6:3

Christians affirm the transcendence of God. We stubbornly confess that God is radically "other," transcending the categories of human experience. We confess that our ability to conceive of God is always limited by minds that are simply not vast enough to comprehend the vastness of God.

Christians admit that language is just so many words, too earthbound even at their best (which is very good) to speak the deepest truth about divinity. "You can be competent in many things," remarked the late Henri Nouwen, "but you cannot be competent in God."[1]

However (and this is the great however of our faith), we who are Christians dare to affirm that this gulf between our limited humanness and the radical transcendent otherness of God has been bridged by Jesus Christ. Robert Clyde Johnson, in his book *The Meaning of Christ,* observes that this is such a daring affirmation for religious people who have long been insistent about the mystery and transcendence of God that it is "on the ragged edge of blasphemy."[2] Such claims certainly seemed like the ragged edge of blasphemy to many people in Jesus' day.

We who bear his name insist that the Jesus we encounter in the Gospels is like us in our humanity. The Gospels are remarkably down-to-earth in their presentation of this Jewish carpenter who eats and drinks, walks the dusty roads of a backwater Roman province, tells stories about farmers and crafty merchants, loves and heals, and comes to die a criminal's death.

1. Quoted to me by Nouwen's good friend the Reverend Don Postema.
2. Johnson, *The Meaning of Christ* (London: Carey Kingsgate, 1966), p. 10.

Yet the really audacious Christian claim is that in and through Jesus we encounter God in such a powerful way that we dare to claim that this same Galilean peasant named Jesus is God. Paul captured the irony of incarnation in the second chapter of Philippians when he wrote of Jesus:

" . . . who, though he was in the form of God, did not regard equality with God as something to be exploited, but emptied himself, taking the form of a slave, being born in human likeness" (*vv. 6–7*).

Christian affirmation always ends up somehow echoing Fred Buechner's words, "A Christian is one who points at Christ and says, 'I can't prove a thing, but there's something . . . . ' "[3]

But Christians do not believe that the Christ through whom they see into God is precisely the same thing as God. We believe that Christ's words, love, sacrifice, and resurrection reflect the mind of God, yet they do not exhaust the whole mystery of God. Jesus Christ is the fullest expression of God's Word, but this is not the same thing as saying that God can be reduced to Jesus Christ.

3. Frederick Buechner, *Wishful Thinking: A Theological ABC* (New York: Harper & Row, 1973), p. 32.

Through Our Lord Jesus Christ

Therefore, since we are justified by faith, we have peace with God through our Lord Jesus Christ, through whom we have obtained access to this grace in which we stand; and we boast in our hope of sharing the glory of God. And not only that, but we also boast in our sufferings, knowing that suffering produces endurance, and endurance produces character, and character produces hope, and hope does not disappoint us, because God's love has been poured into our hearts through the Holy Spirit that has been given to us.

—Romans 5:1–5

One might speak of Christ as the window through whom we see with clarity into God. What we see through Christ is boundless and self-sacrificing love. In reflecting on how to view modem art, the Spanish philosopher Jose Ortega y Gassett noted that such art is like a window through which we see a garden. If we focus only or mostly on the window—its frame and the glass—the garden beyond is blurred. But if we look through the window (whose function, after all, is to be transparent) to the garden in the distance, the garden comes into clear view, and the window has served its proper function.[1]

The whole story of God is radically condensed in the Trinity. For Christians, Jesus is the center of that story, the crisis and climax of the drama. The whole overarching narrative of Scripture condensed into the Trinity reveals the God seen through the window of the Christ event. What we glimpse is a God whose very nature is love and who can be understood only in and as relationship.

Christians are monotheists; we believe in one God. The prevailing popular image of that one God of monotheism is a solitary being locked in a self-contained, often austere singularity. This popular image is of a God alone and singular in transcendent divinity, whether it is abstracted by theologians and philosophers or sentimentalized by songwriters as the "man upstairs." Though perhaps personal in some sense, in the end

1. Johnson, *The Meaning of Christ*, p. 16.

Knowing God's Triune Story

the God of non-Trinitarian monotheism inevitably drifts toward Miss Thriplow's empty desert or science fiction's stone monolith floating in the cold heart of space.

The story of God summarized in the Trinity, on the other hand, presents an image of God radically different from this imagined God of distant and austere disconnectedness. The story of God in the Bible tells of a being who is passionately and tirelessly longing for and pursuing relationship. The God of the great story shortened to the Trinity is the God who related to the cosmos in the very act of creating it and calling it good. The God of the great story condensed as the Trinity is a God who calls, loves, pursues, grows angry with, and forgives Israel in the narratives of the Hebrew Scriptures, our Old Testament. And in Jesus Christ, "God so loved the world that [God] gave [God's] only Son . . ." (John 3:16). In Christ, God loves us, teaches us, heals us, dies for us, and lives for us. And then, as the great story leads to the threshold of our own lives, God is Holy Spirit, Sacred Wind, the Divine Breath, God in the present tense passionately in us and insistently with us here and now.

Day 19
God for Us

To you it was shown so that you would acknowledge that the Lord is God; there is no other besides him. From heaven he made you hear his voice to discipline you. On earth he showed you his great fire, while you heard his words coming out of the fire. And because he loved your ancestors, he chose their descendants after them. He brought you out of Egypt with his own presence, by his great power, driving out before you nations greater and mightier than yourselves, to bring you in, giving you their land for a possession, as it is still today. So acknowledge today and take to heart that the Lord is God in heaven above and on the earth beneath; there is no other.

—Deuteronomy 4:35–39

The nature of the God who has made God's self known to us in sacred history and in our individual and communal experience is a God who cannot even be spoken of except as God for us. Every act of our God is an extension of the divine self, a reaching out of the divine being toward us in love.

For the Christian, there is central importance in remembering the continuity between what God does and who God is. Christians insist that revelation is trustworthy. There is no hidden God behind the God of revelation, no other God who is essentially different from the God who has encountered us in revelation. We trust that God has loved and does yet love the world. We trust in the continuity between what God does and who God is. This trust brings us to the stunningly radical implication that God is love. Not only does God love, but God is love. God not only longs for relationship outside God's self, but God is—in God's very self, by God's very nature—loving relationship.

Knowing God's Triune Story

"Beloved, let us love one another, because love is from God; everyone who loves is born of God and knows God . . . for God is love. . . . No one has ever seen God; if we love one another, God lives in us, and [God's] love is perfected in us" (*1 John 4:7–12*).

For me, the most transforming affirmation about God imbedded in the Trinity, the towering truth that lies at the heart of that mystery, is an image of God who is love, an image of a God who is relationship, an image of a God who is communion. The ultimate reality of the universe is a relationship of intense love and profound communion.

One in Three Persons

*The grace of the Lord Jesus Christ, the love of God, and the communion
of the Holy Spirit be with all of you.*

—*2 Corinthians 13:13*

Augustine spoke of the internal relationship between the three persons
of the Trinity in which God the Creator is named Lover; Jesus Christ,
the Beloved; and the Holy Spirit, the Love that defines and radiates
from that relationship.

The word *person,* long used to name each of the three parts of the Trinity,
means something different today from when Tertullian introduced it in
the third century. In fact, it has become a problem when used in refer-
ence to God. We tend to use the word and to understand a person as
an independent agent not necessarily connected to other persons. In
this view, a person is a person largely because of his or her individual
experiences, unique thinking, and way of doing things.

The problem with this is that such a notion of self is fundamentally
deficient because our personhood, our very humanity, is invariably
shaped in relationship to other persons. These relationships are not
something added to a fundamentally private self, but are the very
things that have made us into "selves." Our basic nature is relationship,
and our humanness, our personhood, is drastically misunderstood by
defining "person" simply in terms of what goes on inside of us. As the
Scottish philosopher John Macmurray phrased it: "I need 'you' in order
to be myself."[1]

Psychologists have long speculated about how children utterly cut
off from human relationships might develop. Their speculations were
tragically confirmed in recent years when the numerous orphanages of
Ceausescu's Romania were opened to the world's eyes after his fall from
power. The dictator had mandated bizarre policies that had resulted

---

1. John Macmurray, *Persons in Relation* (London: Faber and Faber, 1961), p. 69.

Knowing God's Triune Story

in thousands of unwanted children, many of whom ended up in vast, underfunded, state-run orphanages where they often received no love, no human contact—indeed, where they were not in relationship with other human beings. The children grew into adults who were human creatures, but not human persons. They could not speak or relate to others; they could not receive or give affection. The children were a stark reminder of this truth that is so close to us that we miss it: our very personhood is necessarily shaped in relationship to other persons.

God's Spirit Community

They devoted themselves to the apostles' teaching and fellowship, to the breaking of bread and the prayers. Awe came upon everyone, because many wonders and signs were being done by the apostles. All who believed were together and had all things in common; they would sell their possessions and goods and distribute the proceeds to all, as any had need. Day by day, as they spent much time together in the temple, they broke bread at home and ate their food with glad and generous hearts, praising God and having the goodwill of all the people. And day by day the Lord added to their number those who were being saved.

— Acts 2:42–47

When we try to speak of the three persons of the Trinity in the language of individualized personhood— vocabulary that has forgotten that personhood is essentially relational—the word makes little sense. Andrew Purvis summarized the problem this way:

"What does it mean to say that God is a person, that God is personal being, or that God is a self? Is God's self constituted by God's self-awareness, experiences, feelings? And more problematic yet: How can God be three persons if that means three individuals, three distinct subjects of experience and consciousness?"[1]

The alternatives are obvious: either we don't talk about God as person, or we expand and mature our understanding of personhood in a dramatic way that encompasses the reality that personhood is fundamentally relational. In this view, difficult for children of an age of radical individualism to grasp, the three persons of the Trinity are seen not as individuals, but as participants in an abiding and eternal relationship of love. (Love can be love only if there is relationship.)

In 1989, the British Council of Churches issued a study paper titled "The Forgotten Trinity" in which this ancient "social doctrine of the Trinity" is presented in such a way as to affirm that God is a community

---

1. Quoted in an unpublished series of lectures by Andrew Purvis, Montreat Conference Center, summer 1996.

consisting in "unbroken personal relationships."[2] Catherine LaCugna, a contemporary theologian of the Trinity, puts it this way: "Only in communion can God be what God is, and only as communion can God be at all."[3] To imagine God as an unbroken, abiding communion of intense—indeed, passionate—love is in the happiest and most profound contrast with all of our struggles to imagine God as radically alone, as an empty desert, or a block of stone, or an angel alone on a cloud.

Precisely what the book of Genesis may mean when it says that you and I were created "in the image of God" has long evaded biblical scholars. I think it means that we are human only in relationship, just as God is God only in relationship. Such an understanding has far-reaching implications for how people who would follow God should live. It implies nothing less than this: the essence of that which is "of God" is everything that promotes, nourishes, deepens, and sustains relationships of love, trust, and intimacy.

Likewise, it also implies nothing less than this: demeaning, trivializing, or severing such relationships is an offense against the very nature of God. Such sins are not just disobedience of God's will; they are violations of God's very being.

The unavoidable conclusion is that we who call upon a Trinitarian God are called to live out in our own lives, and to nourish in the lives of others, relationships of deep communion. Such relationships reflect the inner life of God. Our ethics are transformed from simple, dull obedience to a distant God of sovereign power into a quest to conform our lives ever more faithfully to the very life of God.

When the church becomes a community of mutual love for others within the fellowship and active love for the world beyond, it is an incarnation of the love that is and flows from the Triune God.

 On the following page write down three things you wonder about the Trinity that are not addressed by the readings this week.

2. "The Forgotten Trinity," in *A Study Guide on Issues Contained in the Report of the BCC Study Commission on Trinitarian Doctrine Today* (London: Inter-Church House, 1989), p. 16.
3. Catherine Mowry LaCugna, *God for Us* (San Francisco: HarperSanFrancisco, 1991), p. 260.

God as Love

Main Idea

The ultimate reality of the universe is the relationship of intense love and profound communion that is God.

Preparing to Lead

- Read the daily readings for Days 15–21.
- Read through this session and choose activities and discussion topics. Be open to asking questions that arise from your reading of the book.
- Consider: Augustine said that God is ineffable—that is, beyond utterance, unspeakable—and that we speak of God only to avoid utter silence. With this caveat in mind, explore the question "What do you imagine when you say the word *God?*" Remember that there are different kinds of intelligence, and thus, different kinds of expression, so encourage people to speak of God in the manner that suits them: words, drawings, music, story, metaphor. Pursue the various suggestions made in the material, noting which ones seem more or less helpful. See what consensus, if any, the class can come to, and discuss how your church's worship practice suits or does not suit various people's understanding of God.

Opening Activities

- Welcome: As group members arrive, extend words and gestures of welcome. Consider providing name tags and pens. Give some thought to asking another group member to provide refreshments.

- Read Exodus 20:4–6. Ask: Can a word become an "idol" of God? Could a particular metaphor become an "idol"? Consider the following metaphors commonly used to depict God, and note how each is, or is not, an appropriate image of God's reality.

- ❑ Rock
- ❑ Living Water
- ❑ Dove
- ❑ Father
- ❑ Creator
- ❑ Home
- ❑ Sustainer
- ❑ Light
- ❑ Consuming Fire
- ❑ Bread
- ❑ Sovereign
- ❑ Savior
- ❑ Lover

- Opening prayer: After the previous discussion, invite the group members to join you in prayer.

Guiding the Discussion

- Consider Miss Thriplow (Day 16). The session's description of the fictional character's unsuccessful attempt at meditation on God is amusing, but is it a reliable indicator of the validity of meditation in general? Because one fictional character failed to envision a meaningful god, does it necessarily follow that all meditation not rooted in the Trinitarian formula is equally absurd? Compare Miss Thriplow's meditation effort with that depicted in Psalm 139. There is no "image" of God in the psalm, but neither is the concept of God empty. Why?
- Using dictionaries, explore definitions:

  - ❑ Define the word *sovereign*. Which definition applies to the idea of "sovereign love" as used in Days 15–21?
  - ❑ Define the word *intimacy*. Why is the hope of intimacy pertinent to Days 15–21?

- Ask: How do we see "through" Jesus to know God? Is it possible to see through other persons to know someone else who is related to them in some way? Describe how one might see through a child to know the parent; through the lover to know the beloved; through the soldier to know the commander; through the student to know the teacher. Could such "seeing through" work in reverse, from parent to child or from teacher to student? Why or why not?

- Consider: The typical child knows the parent only through that parent's relationship with the child. A young child may know nothing of the parent's activities outside the home: at work, in recreation or education, and so forth. In the same way, might it not be possible that although we know God only through God's relationship with us, there might be much more to God that may not involve relationship in any way?

- Ask: If humans can be fully persons only in relationship with others, is it also true that human beings who, for whatever reason, are prevented from forming relationships are not really persons, that they are somehow human creatures but not human persons? What are the moral and ethical implications of defining the boundaries of personhood in such a way that certain humans are considered persons who are not human?

Concluding the Session

- Invite a participant who enjoys reading to read Psalm 107 aloud to the group. Invite the other participants to close their eyes and relax, allowing any images to come to their minds that the psalm evokes. Allow a moment of silence after the reading, and then encourage group members to share any impressions that came to their minds during the reading. Ask: What particular images or metaphors of God does the psalm suggest? Remember that this is a time for sharing, not for discussion or criticism of others' thoughts.

- Using hymnals, look up the Advent carol "Come, Thou Long-Expected Jesus." How does this hymn express musically what the doctrine of the Trinity expresses in words alone? What is the emotional content of this carol? How does it capture the threefold experience of God common to Christians since the beginning of the church?

Notes:

Credo

Day 22
John 1:1-14

In the beginning was the Word, and the Word was with God, and the Word was God. He was in the beginning with God. All things came into being through him, and without him not one thing came into being. What has come into being in him was life, and the life was the light of all people. The light shines in the darkness, and the darkness did not overcome it.

There was a man sent from God, whose name was John. He came as a witness to testify to the light, so that all might believe through him. He himself was not the light, but he came to testify to the light. The true light, which enlightens everyone, was coming into the world.

He was in the world, and the world came into being through him; yet the world did not know him. He came to what was his own, and his own people did not accept him. But to all who received him, who believed in his name, he gave power to become children of God, who were born, not of blood or of the will of the flesh or of the will of man, but of God.

And the Word became flesh and lived among us, and we have seen his glory, the glory as of a father's only son, full of grace and truth.

Prayer:

> God Most High,
> your only Son embraced the weakness of flesh,
> to give us power to become your children;
> your eternal Word chose a dwelling among us,
> that we might live in your presence.
> Grant us a spirit of wisdom
> to know how rich is the glory you have made our own,
> and how great the hope to which we are called
> in Jesus Christ, your Word made flesh,
> who lives and reigns with you in the unity of the Holy Spirit,
> in the splendor of eternal light,
> God forever and ever. Amen.[1]

---

1. *Book of Common Worship* (Louisville: Westminster John Knox Press, 1993), p. 187. Reprinted with permission of the Office of the General Assembly.

Knowing God's Triune Story

Trinity in the Bible

Does not wisdom call,

and does not understanding raise her voice? . . .

The Lord created me at the beginning of his work,

the first of his acts of long ago.

—Proverbs 8:1, 22

The word *Trinity* never appears in the Bible; so how did it come to be that Christians confess a God who is "three in one" and end their prayers by saying "in the name of the Father, and of the Son, and of the Holy Spirit"? How has it come to be that most of the historic creeds that we affirm are Trinitarian in both shape and content?

One of the objections to the doctrine of the Trinity has been that it is not biblical. In one sense, this observation is valid. Not only does the word never appear in Scripture, but nothing like the doctrinal formula "one God in three persons" is ever used by any of the biblical writers. It is true that the Trinity is not explicit in the pages of Scripture.

But it is equally true that the doctrine of the Trinity is inescapably implicit in the Bible. This is true at two levels. First, the biblical story tells us of a God who is present to us in history and experience:

- as Creator and God of Israel, the God whom Jesus knows as Abba,
- as the creative and expressive Word of God revealed especially in Jesus Christ,
- as the Spirit of God, inspirer of prophets, the Spirit that rested on Jesus in his baptism, the Spirit that comes afresh at Pentecost, the Spirit who is the present tense of God, stirring and comforting us in our time and place.

At this first level, the Trinity is "biblical" in that it is a faithful and radical condensation of the great story of God.

On a second and more specific level, the New Testament often presents a faith, even a theology, that thinks about God and offers praise to God whom the writers understand and speak about as Father, Son, and Holy Spirit. But even in the Old Testament, we hear language about God that often seems to prefigure the language of the Trinity.

The author of Genesis connects the creative act of God at the beginning of time with speech, the expressive aspect of divine nature: "And God said, 'Let there be light.' " God does not "make" light; God speaks light into being. The Spirit of God is mentioned time and again in the Hebrew Scriptures as the formative extension of God who is present (or not present) in the lives of judges, prophets, kings, and Israel itself.

Less familiar to most Christians is the vocabulary of Hebrew thought sometimes used, especially in the book of Proverbs, which speaks of the Wisdom of God in a personified way, much as Christians speak of the Word or the second person of the Trinity. In the eighth chapter of Proverbs, Wisdom herself (the word is feminine in both Hebrew and the Greek) speaks: "The LORD created me at the beginning of [the Lord's] work, the first of [God's] acts of long ago. Ages ago I was set up, at the first, before the beginning of the earth. . . . And now, my children, listen to me: happy are those who keep my ways. . . . For whoever finds me finds life and obtains favor from the LORD" (*vv. 22–23, 32, 35*). Proverbs 8 was a key text in the church's struggle to speak about the second person of the Trinity, the *logos* of John's gospel, the preexistent Christ.

The New Testament

So then, brothers and sisters, we are debtors, not to the flesh, to live according to the flesh—for if you live according to the flesh, you will die; but if by the Spirit you put to death the deeds of the body, you will live. For all who are led by the Spirit of God are children of God. For you did not receive a spirit of slavery to fall back into fear, but you have received a spirit of adoption. When we cry, "Abba! Father!" it is that very Spirit bearing witness with our spirit that we are children of God, and if children, then heirs, heirs of God and joint heirs with Christ—if, in fact, we suffer with him so that we may also be glorified with him.

—Romans 8:12–17

Two of the books of the New Testament that scholars believe were written very early in the life of the church begin to explore God in ways that infer a God who is three, yet one. In the second chapter of 1 Corinthians, Paul summarizes his message for his readers. He begins with the mystery of God, then moves to Christ crucified, and in the rest of the summary, speaks of the Spirit through whom God reveals these things to us.

In the second chapter of his letter to the Philippians, Paul encourages his readers in the Christian way of life by speaking of Christ and the Spirit. He then quotes what may have been an old Christian hymn or confession of faith that outlines the relationship between God and Jesus Christ: ". . . who, though he was in the form of God, did not regard equality with God as something to be exploited, but emptied himself, taking the form of a slave, being born in human likeness. And being found in human form, he humbled himself . . . " (*vv. 6–8*).

In the profound and complex theology of the eighth chapter of Romans, Paul speaks of God in the language of Father, Son, and Holy Spirit:

"When we cry 'Abba! Father!' it is that very Spirit bearing witness with our spirit that we are children of God, and if children, then heirs, heirs of God and joint heirs with Christ . . . . " (*vv. 15–17*).

The most developed pre-Trinitarian thinking about God in the New Testament comes, however, in books written just a few years later. The first chapter of the letter to the Ephesians is veritably Trinitarian in its outline. But the clearest and most winsome whispers of the Trinity are in the Gospel according to John. The profound words of the first chapter of John's Gospel, particularly the prologue (*John 1:1–18*), describe in a style both theological and poetical the relationship between the Creator God and the Word of God. The expressive, active Word of God was first in creation and is now in Jesus Christ: "In the beginning was the Word, and the Word was with God, and the Word was God. . . . All things came into being through him . . . . And the Word became flesh and lived among us, and we have seen his glory, the glory as of a father's only son, full of grace and truth" (*John 1:1, 3, 14*).

In the third chapter of the Gospel according to John, in response to a question from a curious Pharisee named Nicodemus, John unfolds what is perhaps the most nearly Trinitarian theology in all of the New Testament. The answer offered to Nicodemus' naive question "How can anyone be born after having grown old?" speaks of God in the language of God and Christ, reaching a crescendo in the familiar verse 16: "For God so loved the world that [God] gave [God's] only Son . . . ."

Day 25
The Holy Spirit

"The wind blows where it chooses, and you hear the sound of it, but you do not know where it comes from or where it goes. So it is with everyone who is born of the Spirit."

—*John 3:8*

In the Nicodemus story, the identity of each person of the Trinity is quite in line with later Trinitarian theology. The Spirit is the power and presence of God in our midst, in the moment, active and sensed, like the wind. The Son is the one whose ministry makes this possible. He is the light, the incarnation, the one who descends from heaven. The God who so loved the world is in heaven: God in God's self. The love that animates this story is, of course, the main verb of later Trinitarian theology. This includes both God's love for the world (the economic Trinity) and love as the essential relationship within the Trinity (the immanent Trinity). This, too, is a central theme for John in his emphasis on the relationship of profound love between Jesus and the God whom Jesus names Father, as well as on God's love for the world and Jesus' love for his disciples.

Later, in the fourteenth through the seventeenth chapters of John, as the cross shadows the end of his earthly ministry, Jesus is in intimate fellowship with his followers. He speaks at length about his relationship to them, and to the Father, and to the Spirit: "If you love me, you will keep my commandments. And I will ask the Father, and [the Father] will give you another Advocate, to be with you forever. This is the Spirit of truth . . . . You know [the Spirit], because [the Spirit] abides with you, and . . . will be in you" (*John 14:15–17*).

New Testament Trinitarian Formulas

"Go therefore and make disciples of all nations, baptizing them in the name of the Father and of the Son and of the Holy Spirit, and teaching them to obey everything that I have commanded you. And remember, I am with you always, to the end of the age."

—*Matthew 28:19–20*

Two New Testament books conclude with a Trinitarian charge or blessing. The Gospel of Matthew ends with the Great Commission: "Go therefore, and make disciples of all nations, baptizing them in the name of the Father and of the Son and of the Holy Spirit" (*28:19*). Paul draws his correspondence with the Corinthians to a close with what has become known as the apostolic benediction, in which the order of the Trinity is presented distinctly: "The grace of the Lord Jesus Christ, the love of God, and the communion of the Holy Spirit be with all of you" (*2 Cor. 13:13*).

In the story of Jesus told in the Gospels, there is one grand scene in which all three persons of what would later be called the Trinity are present and on stage together: the baptism of Jesus by John. First, the Spirit descends upon the scene "like a dove . . . alighting upon him." Then God the Father speaks offstage in a voice deeper than hearing, focusing all eyes and ears on the figure at center stage: "This is my Son, the Beloved, with whom I am well pleased" (*Matt. 3:17*).

Questions arose immediately. Paul's letters, written in the three decades after Christ's death and resurrection, were, in most cases, written in response to theological discussions and disputes in the churches he had started. From the earliest days, a certain Christian diversity was the rule. The early church comprised not only ethnic variety but also diversity in theology, worship, and canon—that is, diversity regarding which Christian writing should be authoritative.

As in modern times, a key question in those days was: What are the limits of diversity? Perhaps the most lasting sign of the early church's graceful accommodation of substantial diversity is the fact that four different Gospels were welcomed into the canon of the church's New

Testament. How tempting it must have been to choose just one or to edit the four into a standard Gospel! How much neater that would have been! This option was, in fact, attempted but rejected. On the other hand, the same church that welcomed four different Gospels excluded other gospels and letters it felt were unfaithful to the event of Jesus.

The story of Jesus of Nazareth is the narrative of what God has done for us. His singular life lived in perfect, incarnate intimacy with God is a sign for human life. Each of the four Gospel writers writes from a particular theological point of view. Even though their narrative is theologically shaped, the Gospel writers generally tell the story rather than draw theological conclusions or doctrines. It naturally fell to the church in the centuries that followed to wrestle with the theological questions that grew out of the Gospel narrative.

Jesus, Divine and Human

Let the same mind be in you that was in Christ Jesus, who, though he was in the form of God, did not regard equality with God as something to be exploited, but emptied himself, taking the form of a slave, being born in human likeness. And being found in human form, he humbled himself and became obedient to the point of death—even death on a cross. Therefore God also highly exalted him and gave him the name that is above every name, so that at the name of Jesus every knee should bend, in heaven and on earth and under the earth, and every tongue should confess that Jesus Christ is Lord, to the glory of God the Father.

—Philippians 2:5–11

Two especially persistent and troubling theological issues faced the early church. First, what was the nature of the relationship of Christianity to other religions and cultures? Specifically, what was the church's relationship to Judaism on the one hand, and to popular Greco-Roman paganism and mystery religions on the other? Second, how did the divine and human come together in Jesus? What was his relationship to God? This second issue—complex, stubborn, and often divisive—was what led Christians to think long and hard about Father, Son, and Holy Spirit and to build the theology of the Trinity.

Theological speculations about the exact nature of Christ's relationship to God had bloomed like a yard full of dandelions after a June rain in the first several centuries of the church's life. Fanciful theories tested the limits of theological diversity and led in time to the writing of creeds, baptismal symbols, and other statements defining the church's core belief and teaching.

Christians in the first four centuries of the church's life struggled to comprehend the implications of the story of the God who had spoken in Jesus Christ. Was Jesus the same as God? Was he like God? Was he just a wise teacher? Was he equal to God or less than God? As conflict reached crisis, it led to the shaping of the explicit doctrine of the Trinity that was implicit in Scripture. As is often the case with crises, these centuries of debate and crisis eventually bore bountiful theological fruit.

In the year A.D. 325, the Emperor Constantine, who had been converted to Christianity, called a council of the bishops of the empire to meet at Nicea, a small town near Constantinople, and charged them with the responsibility of resolving this theological issue. Never before had an emperor assumed such a role in the affairs of the church.

Constantine understood that this was a religious question with dangerous political implications for his fractious empire. Some three hundred bishops attended.

Athanasius emerged as an articulate advocate of a high understanding of Christ as God's very Word and incarnate presence with us. This first great council of the church, the Nicene Council, produced a statement of faith that became the forerunner of our Nicene Creed. In the end, all but Arius and two bishops voted in favor of the creed.

Nevertheless, the conflict continued to rage over the next decades. Struggling to resolve the issue and to think about God in ways that were faithful to the Bible, three great theologians emerged. The profundity and sophistication of their work plumbed the idea of the Trinity to new depths. These three thinkers, Basil of Caesarea, Gregory of Nazianzus, and Gregory of Nyssa, are called the Cappadocian Fathers because they all made their home in that region of eastern Asia Minor. Their work was affirmed by the Council of Constantinople meeting in 381. This second great council of the church produced the creed we now name Nicene, an expanded version of the earlier statement of faith and a fully Trinitarian affirmation of faith.

Day 28
A Trinity of Intimate Relationship

"I still have many things to say to you, but you cannot bear them now. When the Spirit of truth comes, he will guide you into all the truth; for he will not speak on his own, but will speak whatever he hears, and he will declare to you the things that are to come. He will glorify me, because he will take what is mine and declare it to you. All that the Father has is mine. For this reason I said that he will take what is mine and declare it to you."

—John 16:12–15

In recent years, some in the church have experimented with Trinitarian language in response to concerns about the male imagery of Father and Son. We may affirm that God is beyond gender, but "Father-Son" language gives the impression that God is implicitly or explicitly understood as male, especially to the young.

All God language is metaphorical. Over the centuries, Christians have insisted that God is beyond any categories of human gender. Christ came into the world as a male human being; we do not know why. It was not because God is a male human being. Perhaps it had something to do with the cultural constraints of a patriarchal world.

Whatever is the case, the eternal Word of God, the Christ who reigns in the Godhead, is beyond gender. And Jesus, again in the context of first-century Judaism, spoke intimately of God as Father, a familiar term of deep affection and spiritual proximity that could be so heard by his hearers. Fatherhood imputes personal intimacy to God, not gender.

Innovative Trinitarian language such as recent formulas like "God the Creator, Redeemer, and Sustainer" is an attempt to preserve ancient truth while emphasizing that the transcendent God is neither male nor female. Such vocabulary, while perhaps expanding our vision of God, can never replace the ancient words that keep us who live in this one niche of time and in one particular culture in continuity and fellowship with the church universal. We must also guard that such innovative language does not fall into theological mistake by focusing on the activity of the Godhead rather than on its inner relationship of intimate love.

To say that God is a Trinity of intimate relationship is to say that God already exists in the kind of relationship to which God wants to bring us. As Augustine said, "The Holy Spirit . . . makes us dwell in God, and God in us. But that is the effect of love. So the Holy Spirit is God who is love."[1]

 What questions do you want to ask your group about the economic Trinity and the immanent Trinity?

1. Alister E. McGrath, *Historical Theology: An Introduction to the History of Christian Thought* (Hoboken, NJ: Wiley-Blackwell, 1998), pp. 67–68.

**Group
Session Four**

Credo

Main Idea

The doctrine of the Trinity is an affirmation that the church makes in universal agreement, confessing itself as a fellowship bridging the boundaries of time, geography, race, class, language, and culture, reflecting the form of God revealed in the Scriptures.

Preparing to Lead

- Read the daily readings for Days 22–28.
- Read through this session and choose activities and discussion topics. Be open to asking questions that arise from your reading of the book.

Opening Activities

- Welcome: As group members arrive, extend words and gestures of welcome. Consider providing name tags and pens. Give some thought to asking another group member to provide refreshments.
- Invite the group to experiment with describing the Trinity with language different from the traditional "Father, Son, and Holy Spirit." For instance, "Creator, Redeemer, and Sustainer" is gender-inclusive while expressing the relation of each person of the Trinity to the believer. Name further possibilities; then consider what each expresses about God, what each does not express, how each is based in Scripture, and how each might be perceived by different groups of people.
- Opening prayer: After a brief discussion, invite the group members to join you in prayer.

Guiding the Discussion

- Look through each of the following Scripture passages and determine whether they suggest the doctrine of the Trinity (and if so, how). This exercise may be done in small groups.

  ❑ Genesis 18:1–8
  ❑ Deuteronomy 6:4–9
  ❑ Job 19:25–27
  ❑ Isaiah 40:6–11
  ❑ Matthew 3:13–17
  ❑ Luke 24:49
  ❑ John 3:31–36
  ❑ John 7:14–18, 37–39
  ❑ Acts 11:15–18
  ❑ 1 Corinthians 2:1–5

- Consider: What would have been the advantages of having one standardized Gospel instead of four separate Gospels that differ in many ways? What would have been the disadvantages? Why might the early church have decided against a single standardized Gospel in favor of including in the canon the four present Gospels?
- Consider the following groups of texts from the Scriptures. What is the specific function or action of the Holy Spirit in each?

  ❑ Genesis 1:2; 6:3; 41:38
  ❑ Judges 3:10; 1 Kings 18:12; Job 33:4
  ❑ Isaiah 48:16; 63:14
  ❑ John 3:5; 16:13
  ❑ Ephesians 1:13; Philippians 2:1
  ❑ 1 Peter 1:2; 1 John 5:6; Revelation 2:29

- Read Proverbs 8. What is revealed about this "person" called Wisdom? How is Wisdom similar to Christ? How is she similar to the Holy Spirit? Compare also Luke 7:35 and 11:49.

Concluding the Session

- Invite someone who enjoys reading to read the following series of questions to the group. Invite the other participants to close their eyes, relax, and let their thoughts flow freely. Allow a moment of silence after the reading, and then invite group members to share their thoughts. Remember that this is a time for sharing, not for discussion or critique of others' thoughts.

❑ How would your life have been different if you had been taught to pray in the name of the Mother, Child, and Guardian Spirit as well as in the name of the Father, Son, and Holy Ghost?

❑ How would your life have been different if the names of Mary Magdalene, Susanna, Lydia, and Priscilla were included in the lists of the apostles along with the names of Peter, James, John, and Paul?

❑ How would your life have been different if the portraits of revered pastors and elders along the church hallways had included portraits of women as well as men?

• Using hymnals, look up the hymn "Love Divine, All Loves Excelling." How does this hymn express the doctrine of the Trinity? How does it depict aspects of God that are associated with the Creator? With the Redeemer? With the Spirit? What do worshipers learn about the Trinity as they sing this hymn?

Notes:

From God and Back Again

Day 29
John 14:1-11

"Do not let your hearts be troubled. Believe in God, believe also in me. In my Father's house there are many dwelling places. If it were not so, would I have told you that I go to prepare a place for you? And if I go and prepare a place for you, I will come again and will take you to myself, so that where I am, there you may be also. And you know the way to the place where I am going." Thomas said to him, "Lord, we do not know where you are going. How can we know the way?" Jesus said to him, "I am the way, and the truth, and the life. No one comes to the Father except through me. If you know me, you will know my Father also. From now on you do know him and have seen him."

Philip said to him, "Lord, show us the Father, and we will be satisfied." Jesus said to him, "Have I been with you all this time, Philip, and you still do not know me? Whoever has seen me has seen the Father. How can you say, 'Show us the Father'? Do you not believe that I am in the Father and the Father is in me? The words that I say to you I do not speak on my own; but the Father who dwells in me does his works. Believe me that I am in the Father and the Father is in me; but if you do not, then believe me because of the works themselves."

Prayer:
> Almighty God,
> your Son Jesus Christ
> is the way, the truth, and the life.
> Give us grace to love one another,
> to follow in the way of his commandments,
> and to share his risen life;
> who lives and reigns with you and the Holy Spirit,
> one God, now and forever. Amen.[1]

1. *Book of Common Worship* (Louisville: Westminster John Knox Press, 1993), p. 329. Reprinted with permission of the Office of the General Assembly.

God Moves Toward Us

"I have much to say about you and much to condemn; but the one who sent me is true, and I declare to the world what I have heard from him." They did not understand that he was speaking to them about the Father.

—*John 8:26–27*

The story of God is truly but briefly told as the Trinity. The very being of the God who is love is the Trinity. God comes toward us in a movement that is Trinitarian in its progression.

To begin with, there is God, complete, eternal, and transcendent. God forsakes splendid isolation and comes into our time and space. The infinite and eternal Spirit moves to us in our own form so that we may know God in the only language we understand: the language of human life and experience. This step in this divine movement toward us is the story of Jesus, a man who lived nearly two thousand years ago. This is the same Jesus Christ that we confess to be God and human. The meaning of his word and the power of his person became immediate to human beings through the Spirit. God's wind blows through our lives; God's breath breathes on our days. In the Spirit, God moves as near as near can be in this three-step embrace done out of boundless love. God moves from pure divinity into our humanity in Jesus. The Spirit then brings God in Christ into our present lives, the final embrace of the Lord of the Dance.

Prayer:
O blessed Trinity,
in whom we know the Maker of all things seen and unseen,
the Savior of all both near and far:
By your Spirit enable us so to worship your divine majesty,
that with all the company of heaven
we may magnify your glorious name, saying:
Holy, holy, holy.
Glory to you, O Lord most high. Amen.[1]

1. *Book of Common Worship* (Louisville: Westminster John Knox Press. 1993), p. 348. Reprinted with permission of the Office of the General Assembly.

Trinity in Worship

The grace of the Lord Jesus Christ, the love of God, and the communion of the Holy Spirit be with all of you.

—2 Corinthians 13:13

The very shape of Christian worship reflects the Trinitarian nature of God. In most Christian traditions, worship begins with some form of acknowledgment of our incompleteness and our need for God, a hunger that is quickened by the Holy Spirit at work in us. In the Reformed tradition, it is a custom so routine that we miss its familiar significance. Worship moves from opening praise in song and prayer immediately and rather precipitously to another mood: that of the weekly (and often banal) prayer that rehearses the reality of human sin. Our human lack of faithfulness is in sharp contrast to the entirely trustworthy God of Abraham and Sarah. God's faithfulness highlights our unfaithfulness. In truth, our prayer of confession should be less a unison laundry list of the week's assorted omissions and commissions, and more a frank acknowledgment of our restlessness, aimlessness, and brokenness apart from God. All journeys begin with a reason to go; we come to worship because there is an emptiness in us, a void that only the Spirit can fill.

From this beginning in the Holy Spirit, worship moves through Christ. Worship moves through the reading of Scripture, especially the weekly reading from the Gospels, these stories of Christ. Then it moves through sermon in which (by the grace of God) a mortal preacher tries to represent the Word in words. The sermon is not an end in itself (God help us!) but a pointing to Christ in words. Then, on many Sundays worship moves through the Sacraments of Baptism and Communion. These sacred dramas help us remember and reenact the love and grace of Christ.

The pastor stands at the front of the sanctuary, an infant in her arms, or a new adult believer on his knees before the water in the baptismal font. This is the gateway to the faith, the step across the threshold that leads a person on a journey in faith, a journey back to the God from whom we have come. Another great prayer of thanksgiving is offered, a prayer in three parts. And then as water touches flesh (with present water commemorating long-ago water), the name of this child of God and the very name of God are spoken together in the same sentence: "Sara Rebecca Jones, I baptize you in the name of the Father, and of the Son, and of the Holy Spirit."

Day 32
At the Lord's Table

When he was at the table with them, he took bread, blessed and broke it, and gave it to them. Then their eyes were opened, and they recognized him; and he vanished from their sight. They said to each other, "Were not our hearts burning within us while he was talking to us on the road, while he was opening the scriptures to us?"

—Luke 24:30–32

The pastor stands at the front of the church, behind a table that doesn't look like anyone's breakfast table. Only bread and wine grace this table, a meal for the hungry soul. This is a meal that becomes a ceremony to commemorate and to re-create another meal set and eaten two millennia ago. It is a meal with words, the same words again and again, week after week, year after year, century after century. The words recall the life and invoke the presence. "The Lord be with you," the pastor begins. "And also with you," the gathered people answer yet another time.

The story unfolds yet again from the far side of the table, a story told in three parts, a story told in a prayer of thanksgiving, as if the Almighty needed reminding. "In your wisdom you made all things and sustain them by your power. You commanded light to shine in the darkness, divided the sea and dry land, created the vastness of the universe and called it good. You made us in your own image to live with one another in love. When sin scarred the world, you entered into covenant to renew your creation. As a mother tenderly gathers her children, as a father welcomes home his own, you embraced Israel, a whole people, as your own and filled them with a hunger for peace and justice. Through the words of the prophets you promised your people a redeemer and gave hope for that day when justice shall roll down like waters, and righteousness like a living stream." That's God the Father, the Creator and source of all power and majesty.

The second part of the story follows: "You raised up Jesus, your Son, the Living Bread, in whom ancient hungers have been satisfied. . . . We praise you, most holy God, for sending your Son to live among us, sharing our joy and sorrow. He told your story, healed the sick, and was a friend to sinners. He overcame death and is risen to rule the world and is still a friend to sinners. . . ."

The pastor touches the bread and the wine. She lifts them up and holds them before our eyes—fresh bread and new wine—here, present, real. We may taste and eat. This is not memory; it is now. This is not distant history; it is present reality.

The pastor then says: "Gracious God, pour out your Holy Spirit upon us and upon these gifts of bread and wine, that the bread we break and the cup we share may be the body and blood of Jesus Christ. By your Spirit make us one with Christ, that we may be one with all who share this feast, united in ministry in every place. . . ."

In the very flow of this great prayer of thanksgiving—perhaps the most ancient prayer form of the faith, save the Lord's Prayer—the three-part movement of God toward us in love is spoken, enacted, and made tangible. In the elements of bread and wine, memory becomes present reality in the lives of living men and women.

Worship choreographs our movement through Christ and always toward God, the eternal God toward whom Christ points and leads us. And the very goal of worship is fulfilled when the eternal God is finally met in sacrament, prayer, and our offering of self and substance to God.

Day 33
The God of Ordinariness

Rejoice in the Lord always; again I will say, Rejoice. Let your gentleness be known to everyone. The Lord is near. Do not worry about anything, but in everything by prayer and supplication with thanksgiving let your requests be made known to God. And the peace of God, which surpasses all understanding, will guard your hearts and your minds in Christ Jesus.

—Philippians 4:4–7

We meet God not only in the sacred space of worship, but also (perhaps more so) in the fabric of daily life illumined by the light of Christ. God, met in daily life, makes that life sacramental through the love of Christ. We meet God in those whom Christ calls us to serve. We find God in the very place where we started. There God is, in the midst of life itself: in our homes, offices, and classrooms; in the faces of those we love and those who try us; in the ordinary routines of the world that God so loves; in the very flesh that God deigned to take on for us.

Though it is hardly a rule, the most familiar shape of Christian prayer is that prayer offered to God through Jesus Christ in the power of the Holy Spirit. Though it is hardly a rule, the most familiar shape of the Christian life is that life offered to God through Jesus Christ in the power of the Holy Spirit. Beginning with baptism and continuing with the spiritual nourishment of Communion, Christians journey back to God in a mirror version of God's three-step movement toward them.

Our journey back begins as all journeys begin, with some hunger, unnamed longing, or unaccounted-for emptiness. We do not will this; it is mysteriously quickened in us by something unseen. "Our souls are restless until they find their rest in Thee," prayed Augustine. The very author of restlessness is the Holy Spirit, God's shapeless presence. The Spirit pulls us away from self, from self-satisfaction, and from the deadening monotony of sin. The Spirit turns us toward the one who is greater than we are, the one who is beyond the nearsighted horizon of self.

For Christians, that return to God is through Jesus Christ, who is the image of the invisible God, the incarnation of a God who is a being without flesh, without place and time. Jesus is the face of God for Christians, the Word of God spoken in a language we recognize, God in the flesh, space, and time. He is the way to God, the truth about God, and the life in God. To those made restless by the Spirit, Christ gives their journey a map, a route that leads to the one from whom we come, unto whom we return, and "in whom we live and move and have our being" (*Acts 17:28*).

Christq the Center

As they entered the tomb, they saw a young man, dressed in a white robe, sitting on the right side; and they were alarmed. But he said to them, "Do not be alarmed; you are looking for Jesus of Nazareth, who was crucified. He has been raised; he is not here. Look, there is the place they laid him. But go, tell his disciples and Peter that he is going ahead of you to Galilee; there you will see him, just as he told you."

—Mark 16:5–7

Through Christ, the religious journey becomes more than a vague and undirected wandering toward that which has neither name nor face. The Spirit quickens us and empowers us to move into intimacy with God, the kind of intimacy that dares even to call God Father. In the eighth chapter of Romans, Paul writes, " . . . the Spirit helps us in our weakness; for we do not know how to pray as we ought, but that very Spirit intercedes with sighs too deep for words" (*v. 26*). "When we cry 'Abba! Father!' it is that very Spirit bearing witness with our spirit that we are children of God" (*vv. 15–16*).

The shape of this Trinitarian movement, first from God to us and then back to God, places Jesus Christ at the center, the one through whom God has come to us and through whom we find our way back to God. Giving such a centered position to Christ, who is thus well-named our mediator, is a theology in some tension with much of both classical liberal theology and more modern popular theology.

Popular theology tends to understand religion as a direct and unmediated relationship with God. In such thinking, Jesus is subtly altered into one who is only alongside us. Jesus becomes a fellow seeker and a teacher in whose company we and other God-searchers would search the mystical landscape for an inscrutable and ultimately unknowable God. In truth, Christ does indeed stand by us like our older brother or sister and our friend, but he is also the one who has gone ahead. He is not just on the way with us; rather, he shows us the way because he has been there before us. Indeed, he is the way. Any vision of Christian faith that negates the mediating role of Christ soon finds the Trinity an irrelevance, of course. If Jesus is only a teacher, even first among teachers, but not a Savior, we are, in the end, left on our own. We may be alone in good company, but none in that company can do any more than guess where we are going and how we might get there because no one has ever been there.

All of our insecurities and fears can be addressed with this mandate: Trust in Christ as your Savior in whose company we travel as with one who has gone before, has been witnessed to for two thousand years. Here is one example from the tradition of early Celtic Christianity. It has come down to us under the name of "St. Patrick's Breastplate." Perhaps these are his very words. This is a recent translation from the Gaelic by Kuno Meyer:

"I arise today

Through God's strength to pilot me . . .

Christ with me, Christ before me, Christ behind me,

Christ in me, Christ beneath me, Christ above me.

Christ on my right, Christ on my left,

Christ when I lie down, Christ when I sit down, Christ when I arise,

Christ in the heart of everyone who thinks of me,

Christ in the mouth of everyone who speaks of me,

Christ in every eye that sees me, Christ in every ear that hears me.

I arise today

Through the mighty strength,

the invocation of the Trinity,

Through belief in the threeness,

Through confession of the oneness of the Creator of Creation."[1]

Pause throughout this day and offer this text as your prayer.

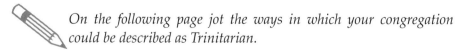 *On the following page jot the ways in which your congregation could be described as Trinitarian.*

1. St. Patrick of Ireland, as quoted in *The Presbyterian Outlook,* May 13, 1996.

From God and Back Again

Main Idea

The sacraments and the shape of Christian worship reflect the Trinitarian nature of God.

Preparing to Lead

- Read the daily readings for Days 29–35.
- Read through this session and choose activities and discussion topics. Be open to asking questions that arise from your reading of the book.

Opening Activities

- Welcome: As group members arrive, extend words and gestures of welcome. Consider providing name tags and pens. Give some thought to asking another group member to provide refreshments.
- Bring out the pyramid sketched on poster board or newsprint from Session 1. Ask participants to rearrange the various components of the pyramid if their understanding of the relative importance of the components has changed. Talk about their reasons for leaving the placement the same or for changing it.
- Ask the participants to form two or more small groups, then pass out recent bulletins from your congregation's weekly worship service. Ask each group to determine which elements of worship might be movements "in," "through," or "toward" each person of the Trinity.
- Opening prayer: See Day 36.

Guiding the Discussion

- Discuss the following quote: "The triune God is the basis of all we are and do as Christians. In the name of this triune God we were baptized. As the baptized ones we bear the name of the triune God in our being. We are of the family of the triune God. We affirm this parentage when, in reciting the creeds, we say what we believe. Our discipleship is rooted in the mighty acts of this triune God who is active in redeeming the world. The triune God is the basis of all our prayers—we pray *to* God the Father, *through* Jesus Christ, *by* the Holy Spirit. The Trinity holds central place in our faith."[1]

- Consider: What is the difference between an ordinary meal that you might eat with family and friends and a meal that has become a ceremony? What other meals, besides the Lord's Supper, could be described as ceremonies? What sets the Lord's Supper apart from all other meals and all other ceremonies?

- Read the entry for Day 32. Consider: How does the prayer of thanksgiving spoken at table express the reality of the Trinity as it retells the story of creation and salvation?

- Ask: Why is the Sacrament of Baptism described as the gateway to faith?

- Discuss the following scenario: Suppose a visitor attends a worship service, then lingers for coffee and doughnuts. During casual conversation, the visitor asks, "What is this business about the Trinity that seems so important to the church? Do Christians worship one God or three gods? Or is three just a magic number?" How would you respond?

Concluding the Session

- This is the final group study session. If there is interest, perhaps the group would agree to meet one more time to discuss the final daily readings.

- Using hymnals, look up the hymn "Come, Thou Almighty King." How does this hymn express the doctrine of the Trinity? What aspects of God are associated with the Creator? With the Redeemer? With the Spirit? What do worshipers learn about the Trinity as they sing this hymn?

---

1. *Companion to the Book of Common Worship,* Peter Bower, ed. (Louisville: Geneva Press, 2003), p. 150.

Three in One, One in Three

Day 36
A Prayer for Trinity Sunday

Leader: Let us give thanks to the Lord our God.

People: It is right to give our thanks and praise.

Leader: Gracious Father,
      giver of all good things:
      For our home on earth
      and for your unfailing mercy,

People: we give you thanks.

Leader: Christ, our Redeemer:
      For your sacrifice on the cross
      and rising from death that we might live,

People: we give you thanks and praise.

Leader: Holy Spirit, giver of life:
      For your abiding presence in our lives
      and for comforting and guiding us,

People: we give you thanks, praise, and glory.

Leader: O triune God:
      To you be glory and praise
      now and forever.

People: Amen.[1]

---

1. *Book of Common Worship* (Louisville: Westminster John Knox Press, 1993), p. 353. Reprinted with permission of the Office of the General Assembly.

Icons and Images

The Lord appeared to Abraham by the oaks of Mamre, as he sat at the entrance of his tent in the heat of the day. He looked up and saw three men standing near him. When he saw them, he ran from the tent entrance to meet them, and bowed down to the ground. . . .

They said to him, "Where is your wife Sarah?" And he said, "There, in the tent." Then one said, "I will surely return to you in due season, and your wife Sarah shall have a son."

—Genesis 18:1–2, 9–10

I have taped an image of the Trinity just above the computer in my study. It is a four-for-a-dollar postcard that someone handed me years ago. It's quite unlike the images of the Trinity I remember as a child. They were geometric shapes fashioned into the dark varnished oak of the pulpit and the trim work behind the choir loft of one of the string of Presbyterian churches my family attended in small towns across Minnesota. I remember a puzzle-like shape formed into wood: a triangle set into a three-lobed circular shape, a mechanical-looking three-leaf clover. Its message was clear; indeed, I still remember it: three, yet one, an oaken diagram of divinity.

The image above my computer screen, on the other hand, is a copy of a fifteenth-century painting, a Russian icon by a master of the form named Rublev. It is called *The Holy Trinity,* though at its first level it is supposed to be a picture of the three visitors who called on Abraham and Sarah by the oaks of Mamre in the eighteenth chapter of Genesis.[1] The story is not really about the Trinity, of course. Abraham invites the visitors to eat and to take their rest. One moment they seem to be just desert wanderers; then they seem to be angels; then they are God. Because they were three, Christians have sometimes thought of them as the Trinity, though neither Abraham nor Sarah nor the writer of Genesis had any such thought.

---

1. Visit www.valley.net/~transnat/trinlg.html to view Rublev's icon *The Holy Trinity.*

In Rublev's icon they are seated at table, tall and slender with strangely long arms. They have wings. One is across the table from the viewer, the others on each side. On the side closest to the viewer is an empty place at the table. The table is white, and its clean expanse draws one's eye. On the table is a chalice, and in the chalice is a lamb—the Lamb of God, of course. My postcard is so small that the lamb is hard to see.

Oddest of all, however, is the perspective of the painting. It's all wrong. I had a drawing class in college and I was good at perspective. In proper perspective, all of the lines of the planes in a picture must meet at vanishing points in the back of the picture or to the sides. In this picture, however, the vanishing point is where the viewer is sitting. Behind the picture is not a point, but infinite space. The world behind the painting is infinitely larger than the world in which the viewer is sitting.

Iconographers are required to study not only painting, but also theology and spiritual discipline for years before they may make an icon. The icon is not an image of God; that would be idolatrous. Rather, an icon is a window into heaven. I like this icon, so strange to my Presbyterian eyes, because it invites me in. Through this window into heaven, I am invited into a heavenly place in which a table is set. And around that table is the God-who-is-love, a God whose being is no isolated and austere unity, but a unity somehow in communion, a God whose very being is love. Not only am I invited into the image by the backward perspective that pulls my eye into eternity, but there is also an empty place on my side of the table, a place set for me, a place set for me at love's table.

The image that Jesus favored when speaking of the realm of God was a banquet. The heavenly banquet will be a great party, a feast with a table spread with good things. There will be good company, but maybe not the sort one would expect. Here the last will be first, and the first, last. Best of all, people as unlikely as you and I will be there.

Day 38
Celebrating Trinity Sunday

Therefore, since we are justified by faith, we have peace with God through our Lord Jesus Christ, through whom we have obtained access to this grace in which we stand; and we boast in our hope of sharing the glory of God. And not only that, but we also boast in our sufferings, knowing that suffering produces endurance, and endurance produces character, and character produces hope, and hope does not disappoint us, because God's love has been poured into our hearts through the Holy Spirit that has been given to us.

—Romans 5:1–5

The triune God is the basis of all we are and do as Christians. In the name of this triune God we were baptized. As the baptized ones we bear the name of the triune God in our being. We are of the family of the triune God. We affirm this parentage when, in reciting the creeds, we say what we believe. Our discipleship is rooted in the mighty acts of this triune God who is active in redeeming the world. The triune God is the basis of all our prayers—we pray to God the Father, through Jesus Christ, by the Holy Spirit. The Trinity holds central place in our faith.

Earliest evidence of celebration of a Trinity feast dates from early in the eleventh century. It gained official standing in 1334.

In celebrating Trinity Sunday, remember that every Lord's Day is consecrated to the triune God. On the first day of the week, God began creation. On the first day of the week, God raised Jesus from the grave. On the first day of the week, the Holy Spirit descended on the newly born church. Every Sunday is special. Every Sunday is the day of the Holy Trinity.[1]

---

1. *Companion to the Book of Common Worship,* Peter Bower, ed. (Louisville: Geneva Press, 2003), p. 150.

Knowing God's Triune Story

Day 39
The Trivialization of Trinity

For most of the history of the Christian faith, the doctrine of the Trinity has been one of those religious truths that most Christians would have understood to be near—if not at—the pinnacle of the pyramid of truth. For most of the church's two millennia of history, in all of its theological and denominational variety, the church has set the Trinity at the heart of its understanding of God. The Trinity has been seen as a mysterious but true description of how God is, how God relates to us, and how we relate to God. Today, however, many Christians, including many theologians, tend to marginalize the Trinity. For many, the Trinity has slid well down the side of the pyramid of truth. In the minds of legions of the faithful, the Trinity has been grouped with less important, even esoteric, doctrines like the bodily assumption of Jesus, or double pre-destination. As such, it has been perceived as a theological antique, historically interesting perhaps, but less than compelling and more or less optional for modem Christians.

This contemporary trivialization of the Trinity is perhaps rooted in two misunderstandings. First, for the last several centuries, we have lived as children of an empirical age, tempted to believe that if we work on any problem long enough, if we research it thoroughly enough, if we think about it hard enough, we are capable of figuring it out and understanding it completely. Whether this brave assumption is true of such things as earthquakes, quasars, microbes, and the human body remains to be seen, but it is certainly not true about God. The Trinity is an empirically nonsensical affirmation that God is one and three; it doesn't respond to such easy optimism about being able to figure out everything, even God. The Trinity, by its mysterious nature, guards the mystery and sovereignty of God—a God whose full reality is always just beyond us. But to an age trained in the relative simplicities of empirical reasoning and naive enough to fancy that there are no other ways to think, the Trinity is met as a theological puzzle: it is obviously bad math, an inscrutable mystery, and a profound affront to the secular doctrine that in the end we will be able to banish all mysteries and make everything quite clear—even God.

Day 40
Trinity Is Biblical

Here, at the conclusion of our forty-day study, we can refute the disconcerting claim that the doctrine of the Trinity is not biblical. We can acknowledge that on a superficial level the assertion is true: the word Trinity never appears in the Bible and only a few passages even mention the Father, the Son, and the Holy Spirit together. But our Reformed tradition counsels us to read Scripture as a whole. And as we have seen, when the whole, overarching drama of the Bible is read, it is a Trinitarian God who emerges from the pages:

- In the Bible, we encounter God who is the Creator of heaven and earth, the God of Israel, the God whom Jesus calls "Father."
- In the Bible, we encounter God in Jesus Christ, the creative and incarnate Word of God who "became flesh and lived among us, . . . full of grace and truth" (*John 1:14*).
- In the Bible, we encounter God present to believers then and now, present to the prophets, to the first disciples, and to us now, God whom we call the Holy Spirit.

The doctrine of the Trinity is not the product of the idle metaphysical speculations of dreamy theologians with nothing better to do. Rather, it is the theological result of the church taking the Bible seriously and thinking long and hard about God.

Hopefully, this study has laid out in an understandable way a case for the radical and practical importance of the Trinity. Will you place the Trinity toward the top of your pyramid of truth?

Prayer:
> Almighty and ever-living God,
> you have given us grace, by our confession of faith,
> to acknowledge and worship the eternal Trinity
> in the majesty of the Unity.
> Keep us steadfast in this faith and worship,
> and bring us at last to see you in your eternal glory,
> one God, now and forever. Amen.[1]

---

1. *Book of Common Worship* (Louisville: Westminster John Knox Press, 1993), p. 349. Reprinted with permission of the Office of the General Assembly.

Coordinating Daily Readings and Sessions

It will be important for the participants to be on the same page, as it were. Consider calling the group together for an orientation to the study at least one week before the first session. During this orientation session, distribute copies of the book to the participants. Prepare a reading schedule for distribution to the group; for example, if your group meets on Sundays:

Sunday, (*insert date here*): Read Day 1
Monday, (*insert date here*): Read Day 2
Tuesday, (*insert date here*): Read Day 3
Wednesday, (*insert date here*): Read Day 4
Thursday, (*insert date here*): Read Day 5
Friday, (*insert date here*): Read Day 6
Saturday, (*insert date here*): Read Day 7
Sunday, (*insert date here*): Group Session One; Read Day 8 . . . etc.

Also note for the group that five additional daily readings (Days 36–40) follow Group Session Five. You may agree as a group to meet a final time after Day 40 to evaluate the book and the study sessions. This could also be a time of worship and celebration for your group.

Leading a Small-Group Study

The session plans include a variety of educational methods; the leader of the group study will have the responsibility of choosing the methods that are most appropriate to your group. Each participant in the group should have a copy of this book and should make a commitment to participating in each session. As you prepare to lead the group study, you will want to:

- Read the daily entries.
- Skim through this study guide, noting any activity that will require preparation.
- Obtain teaching and learning resources recommended in the session plans, such as newsprint and markers, masking tape, hymnals, paper, and pencils.
- Focus on the main idea.
- Prepare the meeting space, based on your leadership style. For example, a circle of chairs is conducive to a leader who seeks to foster an open discussion; chairs around a table offer a good space for writing and discussion; and a lectern facing a block of chairs works best for a lecture presentation.
- Pray for the Holy Spirit's guidance.

Ten Keys to Faithful and Vibrant Small-Group Ministry

(Reprinted from *ideas! for Church Leaders* magazine, summer 2009. Used by permission.)

In *Life Together,* Dietrich Bonhoeffer writes, "How inexhaustible are the riches that open up for those who by God's will are privileged to live in the daily fellowship of life with other Christians! . . . It is grace, nothing but grace, that we are allowed to live in community with Christian brethren."[1] Whether a congregation is small, large, or somewhere in between, small groups offer church members opportunities for experiencing the blessing of Christian community and for deepening faith. Here are ten keys to help you create, nurture, and lead small groups in your congregation.

1. Christ-Centered

Small groups take many different shapes and forms. One thing that separates Christian small groups from other types of groups is the commitment to honor and serve Jesus Christ. If this purpose is not foremost, it's time to rethink the reason for your group. Prayer, Christian fellowship, service in Christ's name, and Bible study are key components of a Christian small group. One or more of these may be emphasized, but the best small groups include all four.

2. Leadership

Because leadership can make or break a small group, create an intentional process for recruiting group leaders. Identify leadership skills in church members and help them discern a possible call to small group leadership. Likewise, be ready to say "no" to someone who wants to be a small group leader, but whose gifts and talents may be better suited

1. Dietrich Bonhoeffer, *Life Together* (San Francisco: Harper & Row, 1954), p. 20.

for something else. If you have trouble finding a good leader for a group, carefully consider delaying the creation of the group until you can secure strong leadership.

3. Training, Nurture, and Support

Once you have selected leaders, train and support them before and during the time they are leading a group. Provide concise, relevant, and inspiring training, and expect the leaders to participate. It is especially important for leaders to understand issues of group dynamics. As they serve, seek ways to nurture their faith through spiritual practices; this will also help them nurture the people in their groups. Offer as much support as possible so they do not become overwhelmed in their leadership role. Help leaders research existing resources and give them guidelines for making good choices of resources. (For samples, check with your church library or local resource center.) It is also important to remember that all study resources and curricula (and leaders, if they teach in the context of the small group!) must be approved by the session or governing body of your church.

4. Parameters

Here are a few things to consider:

> Will the group be open (new members are welcome) or closed (new members are not welcome)? If the group is open, help the group leader and members understand what it means to be a welcoming community when new members join. If the group is closed, make sure other church members understand why the group is not able to include new members. (For example, if the group is doing a short-term Bible study on a challenging topic and needs time to build trust among current group members.)
>
> Is the group short- or long-term? How often will the group meet?
>
> Is this a high-commitment group? Or, is it acceptable for members to only come occasionally?
>
> Will the group be content based (Bible study)? Geographically focused (neighborhood)? Primarily evangelical (everyone invites a friend)? Service oriented (mission at home or abroad)? What are some other ideas for focusing the group's reason for being?

Knowing God's Triune Story

5. Covenant

A covenant is a statement of purpose and parameters that group members fashion together and agree to follow. Because people belong to groups for different reasons, encourage the group members to share their expectations with each other. What are you hoping to get from the group? What do you hope to give? A group covenant is a helpful tool to set and check expectations. Throughout the group's life, revisit the covenant to assess how well the group is fulfilling its purpose.

6. Check-In and Follow-Up

During group meetings, set aside time for sharing what's going on in people's lives. Sharing personal joys and concerns may be difficult for some group members, but in most cases, asking someone for an update on the shared information can mean a lot. Between meetings, consider having coffee with fellow group members who have shared joys and concerns, calling them on the phone, or sending them an e-mail message. That could mean the world to them.

7. Extra

Spend time together outside of regular group gatherings. These special gatherings can strengthen relationships in your small groups. Meet for a picnic, go for a hike or walk, or attend a community event together. A retreat is another great way to foster group cohesiveness.

8. Time

When people come to a group meeting, they are sharing the precious commodity of time with the rest of the group. Group leaders must be prepared to facilitate the group as good stewards of the group's time. Encourage the leaders to plan efficiently for the group's meetings, so that no one feels like their time is wasted.

9. Serve

Find big and small ways in which your small groups can serve your church, your community, and the world. Challenge your small groups to put their faith into action by coming together and serving as God's hands and feet in places that are in need of God's love.

10. Existing Groups

What would happen if your elders saw the monthly session meeting as an opportunity to create one or more intentional small groups? How might session meetings be changed for the better with a healthy component of prayer, study, service, and fellowship? What other existing groups could benefit from the adoption of small-group principles? One more thing: Sometimes the best potential leaders come from existing groups. Ask your current leaders to identify group members who may have the necessary gifts and skills for leading.

Small groups often become the closest collection of siblings in the faith that your church members will ever know. It is in this context that Christ's disciples learn the fine art of loving and caring for one another and for holding one another accountable to the Gospel. Small groups can be a powerful extension of your church's ministry.

The author, Cathy Church Norman, is associate pastor
for congregational life and new member ministries at
Kirk Kildaire Presbyterian Church in Cary, North Carolina.